HOT WET & SHAKING

HOT WET & SHAKING

HOW I LEARNED TO TALK ABOUT SEX

KALEIGH TRACE

Invisible Publishing
Fredericton | Halifax | Picton

Library and Archives Canada Cataloguing in Publication
Title: Hot, wet, & shaking : how I learned to talk about sex / Kaleigh Trace.
Other titles: Hot, wet, and shaking
Names: Trace, Kaleigh, 1986- author. | Couture, Christa,
        1978- writer of afterword.
Description: Revised and expanded tenth anniversary edition, with a new afterword by Christa Couture. | Previously published under title: Hot, wet, and shaking. Halifax, Nova Scotia; Toronto: Invisible Publishing, 2014.
Identifiers: Canadiana (print) 20240361474
            Canadiana (ebook) 20240361482
            ISBN 9781778430466 (softcover)
            ISBN 9781778430473 (EPUB)
Subjects: LCSH: Trace, Kaleigh, 1986-—Sexual behavior. | LCSH: Women with disabilities—Sexual behavior. | LCSH: Women with disabilities—Canada—Biography. | LCSH: Sex. | LCGFT: Autobiographies.
Classification: LCC HQ30.5 .T73 2024 | DDC 362.4092—dc23/eng/20231120 | 306.7087—dc23

Edited by Jules Wilson
Cover and interior design by Megan Fildes
Typeset in Laurentian | With thanks to type designer Rod McDonald

Invisible Publishing is committed to protecting our natural environment. As part of our efforts, both the cover and interior of this book are printed on acid-free 100% post-consumer recycled fibres.

Printed and bound in Canada.

Invisible Publishing | Fredericton, Halifax, & Picton
www.invisiblepublishing.com

Published with the generous assistance of the Canada Council for the Arts, the Ontario Arts Council, and the Government of Canada.

This book is dedicated to my younger self and all our younger selves, to the years we'll spend stumbling toward who we're becoming.

What I have stumbled upon has pleased me most.

—Eli Coppola

Foreword **1**

An Introduction, Dear Reader **13**

A Bag of Dicks **21**

And the Warmth Spread Over Us **25**

Fresh-Faced and Orgasm Free **41**

The Lady & The Butch **57**

Disabled Dyke on a Trike **63**

What's in a Name? My Big, Wide Cunt **73**

Looking for Blood **83**

Queer Fits Right Between My Legs **99**

A Work of Erotica: Fuck Me Anywhere **107**

The Tale of the Wooden Dicks **115**

The Doctor Said **123**

Good Grief **127**

Acknowledgements **134**

Afterword **137**

Foreword

Kill your darlings. I've never taken a writing class, but I know that's an adage that experienced writers say. I have written and rewritten this foreword a million times already, so I can promise you that I've done plenty of murdering. (Does this qualify me as an experienced writer?)

Writing a foreword to a ten-year-old memoir that chronicles your sexual development is a real task, as it turns out. How do I introduce new readers to a younger me? What can I write to bridge the gap between the me of 2014 and the present me, thirty-six years old and still a queer little freak? In most ways, not much has changed. I'm still gloriously disabled, my engagement with the world still mediated by my swaying hips and scissoring thighs. I still spend a lot of time talking about sex, and having it. I still have a tendency toward a radical honesty, and I am still drawn to having shameless conversations about all matters of personal business. This continuity soothes me. And still, some things are markedly different, and that difference has been difficult to write around. Notably, just as I began thinking about this reissue and this foreword, I was diagnosed with terminal cancer. So, the knowledge that I am going to die soon is absolutely different, and that has hampered the writing process, to say the least.

On the day I found out I was dying, I shat the bed. I woke up at five a.m. muttering, "Oh, no. Oh, no. Oh, no." I rushed to the bathroom, shit trailing the length of the hall. My cat, always underfoot, was sprayed. My dog licked her lips with interest. I had consumed four litres of a powerful laxative the night prior, in preparation for what was to be a life-saving surgery. It *was* effective. But the surgery was about to be cancelled. At nine o'clock, the doctor called to tell me that, considering the spread, surgery was no longer viable.

Another way I could tell this story is to say that on the day that I found out I was dying—"Am I dying?" I had asked the doctor. "To be frank, yes," he had said—I hosted a party. I phoned a friend. He called another. She called another. My parents drove in. My brother walked over. Someone brought Thai food. Someone brought a bottle of whisky. Twelve of us sat in my living room for hours, not drunk but not sober. At one point, I was tucked in for a nap. A friend went out and bought an oversized package of toilet paper. I still had diarrhea but had insisted on wearing my most expensive cashmere robe all day. Every time I farted, my friends would hold the length of my robe behind me like a train, and we would collectively rush to the toilet. My brave, genderqueer ladies-in-waiting, and I, their Poop Queen. It was a sombre party, but not without laughter.

Just as my healthcare team began to suspect that I had cancer, my publisher reached out to me about reissuing *Hot, Wet, & Shaking* to celebrate its ten-year anniversary. Under normal circumstances, I likely would have declined this offer. As a therapist, I have felt ambivalent about the book I wrote in my twenties, wherein I describe myself as an expert at blow jobs. My career has changed, and has become one in which keeping my private life private is preferable.

And my ideas about sex have changed too. I wrote *Hot, Wet, & Shaking* as I was just entering into a new understanding of myself as a sexual being. At the time, it was liberating to feel alive in my skin and trusting of my worth for the first time. I wrote myself into a character who was sexually provocative and shameless. It's not an untrue description of me at twenty-five years old, or even me now, but it is one dimensional. As I grew older, I put this character away on my bookshelf and have not been able to think about her without cringing. But the suggestion from my publisher arrived as I was preparing to take time away from my practice to recover from surgery. It occurred to me that stepping away, even briefly, from my work as a couple's therapist might create new room to be curious about my younger self. Now, with a new prognosis and a shortened life span, writing and editing has become a lifeline. Google tells me that a lifeline can be described as "a line used to keep contact with a person (such as a diver or astronaut) in a dangerous or potentially dangerous situation."[1] Dying is dangerous work. The threat of losing myself to grief is always looming. I tug on this line to return to myself. In her brilliant book *Body Work*, Melissa Febos writes, "There is no pain in my life that has not been given value by the alchemy of creative attention."[2] I use this as a guiding principle.

Cringing feels like an overused word, but it is perfect in its viscerality. Reflecting on the memoir she wrote in her early

---

1 Merriam-Webster, s.v. "lifeline," accessed February 4, 2023, https://www.merriam-webster.com/dictionary/lifeline.

2 Melissa Febos, *Body Work: The Radical Power of Personal Narrative* (New York: Catapult, 2022).

twenties, *The Misadventures of Awkward Black Girl*, Issa Rae said, "I wish I had not written that book. As a private person, I'm just, like, 'What was I thinking?' And I was so young and when you write that, that is what exists of me in the literary world, is my twenty-four, twenty-five-year-old self, and who wants that?'"[3] This is exactly what I am sitting with, the awkwardness of having put all of my business out there—from the details of a bad hookup to descriptions of my genitals. I mean, I still love my cunt and its sizable capacities. But, Jesus, I can't believe I wrote about it in a published book?!

Still, I can understand my motivations at the time. To be visibly disabled is to live wedged between being constantly observed and being rendered invisible, and I was writing against that dissonance. There was no outsider exploiting me or asking me to mine my trauma—I was making my own empowering choice to create a disabled character for public consumption, one that looked a lot like me.

But while I grew up, the character in this book did not. I read this exaggerated, static version of twenty-five-year-old me and don't fully recognize her. There's something so familiar but slightly distorted about her, like I am looking into a funhouse mirror and all my proportions are just a little off. I find myself wanting to sit down with her over a beer and laugh about the absurdity of the sexual mishaps she keeps having. I want to offer her a new language, invite her into having a more confident voice, and promise her that she does not need to half apologize for herself all the time. I want to have a conversation with her about her crushes.

I suppose that's what this foreword is for.

---

3 @lostblackboy (Jamal Jordan). "When I interviewed Issa Rae last year". Twitter, 16 Jan 2023. https://twitter.com/lostblackboy/status/1615123053368 721409?lang=en

Hot, Wet, & Shaking is a book about my developing relationship to my body and sexuality as a queer, disabled, cisgender woman. When I wrote the original text in 2014, I was on an evolutionary journey, moving away from a shame-based relationship with my body toward one of ownership, celebration, and pride. This journey is not linear, nor does it end. Loving one's body is not a destination. Instead, most of us live with a great sense of movement, shifting over time, feeling embodied in some contexts, ashamed in others. We can often feel adrift, untethered. This is my experience of my body and of disability. I *do* often feel proud. I wrote, at twenty-five, "I am in love with my body," and I wholly meant it. I do not find it difficult to believe that my body is a good body, or deserving of ease, respect, care, and eroticism. This body has kept me alive, has endured much, has provided (and continues to provide) me with unparalleled pleasures. Just now, my cat jumped onto my lap, purring, and I bent my nose down to her, smelled her soft head, buried my fingers into the expanse of her fur. We blinked at one another, and she's settling in now, our bodies co-regulating. And earlier today, I unearthed my Hitachi from underneath my bed, dusted it off, and found out that it is indeed still the strongest vibrator of all time. So, of course, my body is a good body, able to enjoy so much affection and delight. Yours is a good body, too. I long for all of us—my disabled kin, especially—to trust in the inherent divinity of our bodies, the aliveness of them, while we have them. Disabled people in particular are told in countless ways that our bodies don't deserve to be loved, that we should not even exist. Ten years on, I still believe that writing a version of myself into existence—a joyful, self-loving, sexually desirable disabled woman—was, and is, a radically important act.

When I originally wrote this book, I was building on the work of other disabled activists and writers whose work I had benefited from. Leah Lakshmi Piepzna-Samarasinha, Eli Clare, Loree Erickson, and Mia Mingus were disabled icons to me, people whose work had taught me ways of finding pleasure in my disability that I had not known possible. The work of these brilliant teachers was not easy to find. Writing about disability was considered too niche. I found the representation I longed for only after much searching, even with the added benefit of working in a feminist bookstore. Thankfully, in the last decade, the work of disabled creators has become more sought out and discussed. The disability justice movement has contributed to an explosion of new literature and created cultures of intersectional disability organizing across North America.

Now, *Hot, Wet, & Shaking* is being re-released into a world where many bookstores have a disability section and where a diversity of disabled experiences are represented. Because of the work of radical disabled organizers, dreamers, and culture makers such as Stacey Park Milbern, Alice Wong, Andrew Gurza, Imani Barbarin, Leroy Moore, and Vicky Levack, I now trust that more people have become familiar with us disabled folks as whole, as human, as containing multitudes. There is therefore room in my own writing for more honesty about my complicated relationship to my disabled body. You can see some of this complexity in the new chapters "The Doctor Said" and "Good Grief" that appear at the end of this edition.

I originally wrote "The Doctor Said" in 2015, and I remember how risky it felt at the time to be vocal about some of the hardships of living a disabled life. I had been so invested in being understood as powerful, and feared that showing any struggle at all would bring out the kind of able-bodied pity I had been dodging my whole life and was writing against. But I also remember how good it felt to read that piece out loud and feel a pride in myself for surviving. I feel that pride now as I think about the medical interventions I've endured, and that so many of us disabled folks endure, and I'm excited to republish it here. "Good Grief" I wrote while in the middle of doing chemotherapy, and damn, was I sad! Just drowning in mourning. I couldn't and didn't feel any hesitation about writing about struggle because struggling was all I was doing. Reading it back, I think about how raw and surreal those early days of a terminal cancer diagnosis are. I feel the pain in my writing, how disorganized that time was. But now I am not afraid to have my suffering seen by other people. I've been public about having terminal cancer and have found that grieving publicly heals. We all grieve, and the connections that form when you grieve out loud with others are a salve.

Hot, Wet, & Shaking is also written through an unabashedly sex-positive lens. This was important in 2014. Sex positivity was a new(ish) movement then, one that excited me. Relatively speaking, it still *is* a new movement, and it still excites me. Sex still excites me too, and it continues to be a place where I feel at home. In the act of having good sex (which by my definition requires certainty that I am desired, a sense of play, and a heaping dose of perversion—but I invite you to define it for yourself), all else can fade away and I can feel a radical acceptance of myself. As a disabled person, sex is an escape from chronic pain and ableist assumptions about my body. Like when I swim laps, sex is a place where I trust in my own physicality. In the water, I am strong and competent;

in sex, I am the same. Sex positivity gave me the confidence to understand that you can't "do sex wrong." So, writing as a sex-positive feminist in 2014 was a fit for me and still is.

While I knew then and still know now that *good* sex can be a site of radical healing, I have also spent years now as a therapist, sitting with clients amidst the pain and destruction that can be wrought by sexual violence. The ways in which we hurt each other are endless and devastating. Yet, it does not take away from my immutable belief that, while sex can be contorted into a tool used for violence, it can also be one of liberation. Writing about this complexity, Maggie Nelson says:

> [T]he totalizing conviction that sex, desire, or plea-sure is essentially good, essentially healing, essentially empowering, essentially political, essentially any one thing at all ... I reject it. There are major drawbacks to making an attachment to sex central to any politics, in part because of sex's arguably amoral nature, in part because anything posed as an imperative inevitably invites its rejection, and in part because sex varies in its meaning and importance to people, with that impor-tance fluctuating over the course of a life.[4]

Sex is not essentially good, empowering, healing, or political. We all have radically different experiences of sex and our own sexualities, between us and throughout our lifetimes. *Hot, Wet, & Shaking* is a snapshot of my own sex life at a particu-lar moment in time. It details the ways that I have benefited from feminist, sex-positive ideologies, as well as the ways that

---

4 Maggie Nelson, *On Freedom: Four Songs of Care and Constraint* (Toronto: McClelland & Stewart, 2022).

sex has been healing, empowering, and political for me. This snapshot is a generous offering, and I believe there is some essential good in writing shamelessly about the desires of a disabled woman. And these stories now sit alongside other writing about sex positivity and sexual trauma, disability, and desire that add shape to my own writing and experiences.

When I returned to "Disabled Dyke on a Trike," the feeling of that day returned once more. That encounter was a powerful moment for me, one in which I chose protest over politeness. Here, the me of today and the me of ten years ago are still aligned. I still experience ableism and street harassment. I still rail against it when I can. But the most palpable point of continuity is the desire to protest as an act of kinship. Sara Ahmed writes:

> You do not want those who come after you to have to go through what you went through. A complaint can be experienced as what you do for others. ... No wonder complaint is feminist pedagogy: we often learn about worlds from the worst possible situations. We learn what's wrong when we try to address what's wrong.[5]

I like this notion, that complaining, that noticing, is a feminist act of care for others. To protest, on even the smallest of scales, feels like an act of world-building, for myself and for others. In "Disabled Dyke on a Trike," I "complained" to demarcate what I would no longer tolerate, what I felt no other disabled person should be made to tolerate. I stand on the street beside that younger version of myself, in soli-

---

5 Sara Ahmed, "Why complain?" *Feminist Killjoys*, July 22, 2019, www.feministkilljoys.com/2019/07/22/why-complain/.

darity. Fuck those guys! Fuck all street harassers!

Yet, rereading "What's in a Name? My Big, Wide Cunt," I feel disconnected from my younger self. Or maybe the chapter simply feels outdated, thanks to changes in language that have happened because of the trans rights movement. Reading this chapter, I remember how revolutionary it was to learn the formal language for my genitals. The way that young people of all genders are still taught about their reproductive organs is dripping with cisgender, heteronormative patriarchy. But, reading about my fierce commitment to the term "vulva" or even "cunt" is uncomfortable now. I am a cisgender woman. I love my body and my cunt, sure, but I don't feel a particular devotion to this body part, nor does it feel especially attached to my womanhood. The trans liberation movement has taught me and continues to teach me about the expansiveness of gender. I love this lesson, and I benefit deeply from the way that trans activists have blown wide the restrictive doors of the gender binary. So, it can feel dangerous now to get caught up focusing on the language used for my genitals as a ciswoman. I have a fear that this dialogue could be co-opted by ignorant TERFs. As the trans misogyny of this present moment proliferates, I want to make my position clear: as a cisgender woman, I understand trans women and femmes as my peers. As a disabled person whose body has been medicalized and persecuted, I understand all trans people as my kin. I appreciate the feminism that taught me a new language for my genitals when I was young, and I am grateful that queer, intersectional feminism continues to influence language in ways that make room for all of us.

In 2023, the chapter "Looking for Blood" now brings one word to mind: disappointing (or, maybe "disappointment in the state of affairs"). When I had my abortion in 2011, it felt like I was living in an especially oppressive province. Nova Scotia, with its chronically overstrained and abysmally underfunded health care system, was years behind other parts of Canada. Wait times for a surgical abortion were unimaginably long, and the abortion pill, Mifepristone, was not yet available. Since then, things have improved, both in Nova Scotia and across the country. Mifepristone can be accessed nationally, and abortions are finally available on Prince Edward Island. In her book *Abortion to Abolition: Reproductive Health and Justice in Canada*, Martha Paynter documents how activists have won these battles for access. Reading her work is a balm. However, I still feel distress as abortion becomes criminalized across much of the United States. Stories of the violent suppression of the right to choose grow more commonplace all the time. I can't believe that ten years on it still feels like a radical act to write proudly about my decision to have an abortion. Ten years on, I have grown only more certain about my choice, shored up by the pleasure of being a childless gay aunt (Gay Aunt Kay, they call me; My Little Corruptibles I call them).

We're reaching the end now, and writing this foreword has been the most difficult part. How do I send you off to spend a few hours, a few weeks, with twenty-four-year-old me? I've tried several different strategies. I've quoted writers who I think are better than me. I've detailed my dreams. I even tried writing my own obit to see if that would make sense as a conclusion. None of these ideas were right, and I had to kill them. Because, dearest reader, to tell you the truth, I've been writing this foreword while simultaneously processing my death. I am trying to write a graceful ending that, perhaps, protects us both from this reality. Everything is happening all at once, and, when I'm not writing, I'm moping about, a complete sad sack. My friend asked me what I did yesterday, and I said, "Oh, just my own thing." And when they asked more, I confessed that "my own thing" is just weeping in different rooms while my dog watches and tries to lick my snot. (Let me tell you the truth again: I often let her). So, I'm a bit of a mess, understandably. But I don't really want to leave you here at the end of this foreword, holding the weight of my grief. I don't want my own life to end this way either.

I've had a book on my shelf for months called *How We Live Is How We Die*, by Pema Chödrön. More honesty: I haven't read it. (Instead, I find myself obsessively and exclusively reading YA novels about gay wizards.) Based on the title, I can make some assumptions. I *do* intend to die as I have lived. And damn, I have lived well. Revisiting this text was an excellent reminder of that. I am really fucking queer and have been liberated by queer expansiveness; I am disabled and proud of my resilient body and its adaptations; I love sex and its magic, and I've had a lot of it. Do I hope to die while having a gay orgy with a bunch of queer, disabled perverts? Yes, and I might just orchestrate that.

And I hope that this book might offer you the same kind of reminder. Not to inspire you toward orgies of your own (but if it does, excellent). Rather, I want to remind you of how joyful living is. I hope that being in company with this book offers you shameless laughter, an invitation into self-love, and an appreciation for the fragile brilliance of all our bodies.

Thank you for spending time with me
then, and again, now.

Kaleigh Trace xo

An Introduction, Dear Reader

Dear Reader,
Let me be honest.
I must confess:
I do not know what I am doing here.
I do not know where to start.
I am not sure that I am an expert. I am not sure that I am an author. I am not sure I have a memoir in me, or anything worth saying over the length of 200 pages.
I have never written a book before.

When I imagine people who write books, I imagine Hemingway hunting lions and then propping his feet up on some chaise longue like a boss and jamming out a perfect piece of literature on his typewriter in a single afternoon. Or I see Jeanette Winterson, falling in and out of love and then moodily pouring her broken heart into her work, constructing incredible sentences that make a reader weep while sitting under the grey skies of England. A writer looks like Leonard Cohen in a three-piece suit, passing poetry through his lips. It looks like Michael Ondaatje, teaching us Toronto's history and immigrants' stories. It is Agatha Christie typing, typing, typing in her upper-class boudoir. It is Charles Bukowski fueling his brain and his books with booze.

I am not these things. I am messier than all of that, and Halifax is more mundane. There are no lions here. I am not wearing a suit, just stained jeans. I am not smoking a cigarette or drinking a glass of wine. When I get drunk, I just fall over, and sometimes even pee my pants a little. Smoking irritates my asthma. On my desk are only this laptop and a yogurt container grown mouldy, a few coffee cups with last week's dregs, and a small bundle of lint and gum wrappers pulled out from my coat pocket. There are no windows in this room. And it smells weird, too.

These credentials, full of everyday details and lacking entirely in romance, make me feel nervous and ill-equipped. This space does not feel perfect enough to write a book in. My life experiences do not seem exciting enough to narrate. My underwear is too dirty. My hair is a mess.

However, I should start somewhere. And despite all of my uncertainty, there are some things that I do know for sure.

1. I AM A DISABLED WOMAN.

And I have been for nearly as long as I can remember. In 1995, my family and I were in a car accident. This accident caused me to sustain a severe spinal cord injury. Doctors diagnosed me as having paraplegia, and I spent a part of my childhood in a wheelchair. However, children's bodies, with all of their youthful will, are capable of incredible feats. I was out of my wheelchair within a year, stumbling and slipping and fighting to keep up with all the other kids. Today, I amble around with a serious swagger. It looks a little like I am always dancing. My wobbly two-step gets me to all of the places that I need to go: upstairs, downstairs, and across long distances. I am *in love* with my body: the way my thighs scissor in and out, the way my feet curl and tumble in on one another, the broad width of my shoulders that support me when I trip and fall.

Having this beautiful, disabled body and living in this world with such an obvious difference has shaped me irreversibly. Being disabled informs every single experience I have with every person, every street corner, every building, and every set of stairs. I am, and always have been, constantly reminded that my body is different from "normal" bodies, that it is actually physically impossible for me to conform to hegemonic standards of being. I can't fit in because my legs won't let me. My shattered spinal cord bars me from regularity.

I cannot walk through city streets without being disabled, and so I cannot write a book without being the same. This book will not be about my "perseverance," "courage," and/ or "bravery." Those words, with their implicit condescension, have never felt like friends. Instead, this book will be about who I am, in my entirety. I am a woman, I am disabled, I am queer, and I am an avid eater of eggs, to name only a few of my identities. They overlap and move in and out of one another, criss-crossing and informing me and my universe. I cannot *not* talk about them. I cannot *not* write about them.

2. I AM A SEX-POSITIVE EDUCATOR.

Sex, sex, sex. It is kind of my deal. What this looks like: I teach blow job workshops. Seriously. I am a blow job master, an expert, the top of the top. Once a month, I wave around a big, silicone cock in front of a group of people, and I get paid to have this much fun.

But, of course, that is oversimplifying it. I suppose that on the surface being a blow job expert sounds like a pretty specific skill, one that would perhaps not be applicable outside of my current work environment (I work at a sex shop). You may think this job title and skill set make me seem vulgar (I may be). You may think that this book is not for you. And I guess it may not be, especially if you are my family member and reading a book about my sex life makes you wildly uncomfortable (understandable, and in which case: stop now!). But really, this book could be just the thing for you. And really, so could blow job classes. Because being a sex-positive, feminist sex educator is not really about blow jobs at all.

When I teach those classes, when I go to the shop and talk about sex all day long, when I write a blog post about sex, I am not only talking about the practicalities of doing it. I am not necessarily talking about how much fun sex is, though sometimes I am. I am not necessarily being explicit, though sometimes I am doing that too. Instead, what I am trying to do when I go on and on about sex is subvert the repressive ideas that we are taught about the act of fucking.

Talking about sex is important because we live in a world that is saturated with it. Sex is absolutely everywhere. It is on the sidebar of the website you are looking at. It is on the billboards lining our city streets. It is on commercial breaks and in plot lines. It is the climax, the end goal, the outcome, the problem, and the solution. And, despite its constant and inescapable presence, the image of sex that we are force-fed is both harmful and exclusive.

If I were to believe everything I see, then I would believe that sex only happens between thin people. Only men with abdominal muscles do it. Only women with big tits get to bang. Men and women only do it with each other. Sex is for straight people, and sex only ever happens between two of them, never more or fewer than that. Sex is for white people. Sex is for pretty people. Sex is for able-bodied young people. Sex is spontaneous. Sex involves penetration. Sex lasts approximately 4.2 minutes. Sex happens in bedrooms at night. Sex is predictable.

These insidious images of sex leave out some of the best parts. We are not hearing about how sex can be kinky and subversive and very, very naughty in such fun and consensual ways. We are not seeing fat people get down. We are not seeing disabled people doing it on the regular, neither in their chairs nor in their beds. In mainstream media, we rarely see sexy images of people of colour that don't posit them as an exoticized other. Nor do we see fair and equitable depictions of women's bodies, in all of their curvaceous beauty, experiencing pleasure. We don't see men's bodies being anything other than sexually dominant and capable and sure of themselves. We do not see bodies that refuse to conform to this restrictive gender binary. And we do not get to see that sex can be weird and awkward. We do not see sex where someone accidentally farts. Poop and pee never happen in intimate moments. That moment when we realize that the position we are in does not work, where we get stuck with our legs above our heads, where we trip and fall or gag or barf or stumble or put things in the wrong places: those are all cut out and Photoshopped, removed from our sense of reality.

But sex does not work that way. Sex is weird, and wonderful, and dirty, and awkward, and kinky, and queer, and can consensually happen between all sorts of people, anywhere, at any time of day.

As a sex-positive, feminist sex educator, I find myself talking about the realities of real-life sex all the time. And what I have found is that people think it is really embarrassing. Nobody seems to want to talk about the intricate and human and silly things that happen when we try to stick our bodies together. And so, in response, I talk louder and louder and louder and LOUDER. My mouth gets filthier. I try to push boundaries even further. I want to be even bolder, because the shaming silence that surrounds our collective sex lives is what leads to us all having bad sex. It is why we judge other people's sexuality. It is why we don't know how to respect one another's bodies and one another's boundaries. It is why we don't know what consent looks like, and why sexual assault happens. It is why homophobia persists and why transphobia exists.

I am not arguing that just by openly discussing pussy farts, cum shots, and butt plugs, the world will be a better place, no one will be hurt, and we will all live in a blissful utopia where enthusiastic, consenting orgies abound and we each orgasm every time. That would be unrealistic. However, I do believe that the more we talk about what makes us uncomfortable, the less ashamed and the more open to new possibilities and pleasures we will be. Sex will come to mean something more than putting a penis in a vagina. Beauty will become something more than being cisgender, able-bodied, young, and white. Sexual autonomy and expression will be something that we will all have the right to. And consent will evolve into something that we will all be versed in practising. This is why I talk about sex all the time. Loudly. On principle.

3. THIS BOOK BEGAN AS A BLOG.

Eventually, talking about sex at work every day was not enough. Conversations would begin, thoughts would be provoked, and then the customer would walk out of the store happy, sex toy in hand. I would be left standing there with my mind whirling and wanting more. It felt like I was engaging in unsatisfactory sex with a whole city—the kind of sex where people tell me what they want, I give them what they need, and then it is over before I've finished. And so, rather than going home and masturbating, as one is left to do after having unsatisfactory sex, I began going home to write.

At work, my brain would get turned on. The conversations I had with customers would get me thinking about sex, feminism, gender identity, sexual fluidity, patriarchy, and all the ways that our relationships to our bodies are curtailed by social constraints. Rather than work out all of my questions with unsuspecting clients who were really just trying to make a simple transaction, I would go home and pour my thoughts out into my computer. I would write it all down until I was satiated.

So began my blog, *The Fucking Facts*. Within a year, that blog led to a book deal. Now I sit here slightly daunted, trying to amass all my well-lubricated ideas about sex into a single cohesive volume. Something that will make some sense. Something that will mean a thing or two to someone. Something that will glue together all the mixed-up and jumbled, strong and unwavering, new and exciting ideas that I have about sex and feminism and disability into a single printed piece. I am still unsure of all of the versions of myself and where exactly I fit in this world of identities. I am still working out how I got here. I am entirely clueless as to where this is all going. But here's hoping that in the following stories, we can sort a few things out.

So, let me both conclude and begin it all by saying:

This is my first try.

Be gentle on me.
I will try to be honest.
I will try to be kind.
I will definitely be dirty.

A Bag of Dicks

Something happens to you when you begin working at a sex shop. When sex becomes your bread and butter, it is entirely possible to forget that, for some people, this topic is still taboo. Your boundaries change; your sense of "normalcy" is forever altered. Things happen to you that you thought would never happen: you find yourself explaining queer sex to your grandmother; you casually and without consideration discuss the healing power of orgasms with a stranger on the bus; you descend, with only some discomfort, into the realm of being considered a total weirdo. And eventually it becomes more comfortable there, where you no longer have to conform to obligatory social norms. However, arriving at that point may involve some…stumbles.

I am running late. I am almost always running late, which I believe is one of the inevitabilities of being a classic, type-A, overworked overachiever. I am running late and I am multitasking. Also inevitable. If you are a person who wants to do everything, you must eventually learn to do everything simultaneously.

I would put the phone down if I could. Talking on the phone while in line at the grocery store is, I believe, the epitome of being an entitled asshole. As if the person ringing me through is not really human and does not deserve my full attention. As if the people behind me in line really give a shit about the one side of this conversation I am forcing them to listen to. But right now this phone call is inescapable. It's not even much of a conversation. I'm really just repeatedly muttering "mmm." I can't interject much anyway. It is my most neurotic friend Jason on the other end, and cutting him off now would be tantamount to leaving the toilet paper roll empty, or not filling the stapler, or letting food accumulate in the catcher of the kitchen sink. It would be one of those little things with the capacity to annoy him so thoroughly that it is best to just avoid the act entirely. He is in the middle of giving me a remarkably detailed account of his second date with the woman he has been trying to seduce for months, and I recognize that it is crucial for him to see this narrative through in order to alleviate some of his anxiety. Is it a sign that she said she loved his cooking? Should he text her today or wait two days to avoid seeming too eager? Is there a subtext to the fact that she told him her nail polish colour was called "Killer Flirt"?! I am not expected to answer any of these questions. He just needs to ask them out loud.

On the plus side, I look good today. I took the time to brush my teeth and put on deodorant this morning. I am teaching a fellatio workshop tonight, and so I am trying to pass as an adult woman who knows what she is doing. And while for the most part I do (know what I am doing, that is), I do not always look that way. More often than not, my hair is matted and my T-shirt is on backwards. But today is different. My teeth are clean, and my hair is brushed. I have lipstick on, and it has not yet (I hope) smudged its way onto my pearly whites. I am a woman. I am a blow job expert. I am in control.

Except that I cannot find my wallet, and I just dropped my keys on the ground, and the cashier is looking at me impatiently as I scramble to pay and get out of the way. The woman with her baby in line behind me is also glaring at me, disgruntled and annoyed. I am holding up everybody's day. I wish I could hang up my fucking phone already.

And that is when it happens. I am standing in line, with what feels like 100 frustrated people queued up behind me, with a bored teenager watching me and waiting, and I pull out a big, gleaming, silicone dick. What I think is my wallet is in fact my tool for tonight's workshop. A nice clean dildo, fresh and ready for me to display. Later, I will use this cock to teach anatomy and techniques. Later, it will be appropriate for me to be holding a dildo in my hand, because people will have paid for that, and will have come expecting me to do that very thing. But now I am here, in line at an overpriced grocery store wielding a giant dick while a bunch of upper-class, middle-aged women stare at me, shocked. The baby begins to cry. Is it because I have stolen his innocence? Probably not, but it does feel that way.

"It's for work," I say by way of explanation. As though having a dildo in one's bag for work is entirely common. On the phone, I hear Jason grumble, "You're not listening to me, are you?" In front of me, the cashier continues to stare at me with his mouth ajar and his braces gleaming. I shove the cock back in my bag, find my wallet, grab my groceries, and flee.

This is not a unique experience. Things like this are always happening to me. It seems as though I always have vibrators and condoms, lube and butt plugs pouring from my pockets and bulging out of my bag. Just earlier this week I was caught by a truck driver with one hand down my pants as I frantically drove in circles looking for parking. There was a reasonable explanation for this. I was not just jerking it on my commute to work. I had just short-sightedly decided to test out a clitoral stimulating gel earlier that morning. I had assumed it would do nothing, that its "herbal, aphrodisiac ingredients" were bullshit buzz words that would not really get my clit hard nor my juices flowing. I dripped the tingling liquid onto my stuff, threw my pants on, and headed out the door. Unfortunately, the bottle was true to its word. The tingle set in while I was in the car, halfway to work. But rather than turn me on with its "gentle warmth," it started to burn and burn and burn. It felt like my clitoris was dangerously engorged, like it might actually fall off and I would find a little fleshy nub jamming around down by my brake pedal later. Frantically, I shoved my hands down my pants and started rubbing, hoping to absorb the gel onto my fingers and free my junk from its fiery grasp. That is when the truck driver just happened to look down into my car from his high-up perch in the neighbouring lane—while I was furiously rubbing myself.

I have found myself thoughtlessly reading *A Hand in the Bush: The Fine Art of Vaginal Fisting* on the bus, beside a probably quite nice and now deeply disturbed eighty-year-old gentleman. I have detailed my sexual exploits to my co-worker in a booth at a small family restaurant, forgetting that not everyone talks about ejaculating while they shove mayonnaise and French fries into their mouths. I have showed my dick to a grocery store clerk and have had a truck driver watch me rub my cunt. By now, these experiences are comfortably predictable.

And the Warmth Spread Over Us

When considering my early sexual experiences, it makes so much sense that I have wound up in this line of work. My interest in talking about sex is most certainly linked to the fact that for a long time I was very, very bad at having it. Really. I am not just being modest. I may be something of a pseudo sex expert now, but it has not always been this way. I have, in fact, committed what one would think are remarkably obvious sexual faux pas throughout my relatively short life thus far. And I refuse to believe that all of my slip-ups, mishaps, and total mistakes are my fault alone.

Remember being a teenager? It is a truly awful experience. It is a time in your life that is full of regrettable outfits, actions, and hair decisions. You are riddled with near-constant emotional turmoil and ever-present skin problems. You can't really figure out who you are, what you want, or where you are going. And you smell weird. Or at least that's how it was for me. I hated being a teenager.

As a teen, I was subject to all of the universal teen experiences: the hair, the hormones, the smells. On top of that, I had this whole disability thing to grapple with. I was doubly confused. The already mystifying adolescent changes were accentuated by the stark reality that my body was like no one else's. I did not know any other visibly disabled people. Based on my rural Ontario context, there was no one in the known universe like me. No one else with legs that scissored in barely controlled zigs and zags, or with knees that gave out, resulting in unpredictable falls, or with feet that collapsed inward and dragged loudly against the ground. I was a human anomaly, and I could not figure out what the fuck my body was doing or how it was going to overcome the trials of teenhood. Both my present and my future seemed bleak.

The options for my post-high school, adult future, as presented to me by my immediate surroundings, were fairly homogenous. If I were to follow the trajectory of most people I knew, I would have done one of two options. Option One: marry, help my husband on the farm, and reproduce. Option Two: go to university in the nearest city, marry, help my husband on the farm, and reproduce. Neither One nor Two enticed me much. I could not imagine myself fitting into that framework. Try lifting hay bales with a limp. Try milking cows with chronic back pain. It sounded less than ideal. Plus, I've never liked cows. However, the thing that did entice me was adulthood. I wanted out of high school, out of my small town, and out of puberty. Desperately. So while these fairly normative narratives of what being an adult could look like were unappealing to me, I wanted to discover it nonetheless. And I wanted something different.

This is when I became obsessed with the idea of having sex. All I wanted to do was It. While this is probably a common enough adolescent sentiment, my preoccupation came from a different, more convoluted angle. I was not particularly interested in the act itself. I did not want to have sex to satiate all of my raging teen hormones. It was not that I could not stop thinking about it, nor that I thought it would necessarily feel good. I had never been overcome by any insatiable, physical, lusty urges. I had never even masturbated. No, I wanted to do it for other reasons. I wanted to have sex because I believed it was my ticket into adulthood. I thought it would give me some answers; it was a means to an end. The end, in my mind, was becoming a woman.

This all makes some sense really. I was a teenager in a town that barely knew what the internet was. Okay, many people knew what it was, but it was pretty hard to get, considering we lived amongst the endless, golden corn crops of Absolutely Nowhere. Attempts to access what at the time was called the "Information Super Highway" began with the laborious, high-pitched beeps and squeals of the internet dialing up, and ended with any incoming phone call. Needless to say, I had very little access to radical ideas, to different ways of being, or to any information about sex. Sex was therefore a total mystery to me, something that adults did in big cities like New York or Toronto. Sure, some of my girlfriends were having it with older boys in neighbouring towns, but to me this didn't sound like "real sex." My friends' descriptions of fumbling around in the back seats of their parents' cars sounded more like cumbersome wrestling. I wanted to have what I believed was the sophisticated adult sex that happened in movies. I wanted it to feel meaningful, to have a physical experience that would offer me admission into an imagined club of normalcy and would mark my disabled body as acceptable, desirable even.

While I desperately wanted to have sex, I was terrified of doing it. Given the kind of sex education provided in rural Ontario in the '90s, no one had ever really explained to me how it worked. I knew the basics. I understood that a penis went in a vagina. But I assumed there was more to it than just that. I imagined that both parties had to move around. I imagined a lot of bending over, leg-lifting, and a series of rapid pelvic thrusts, none of which I could do. My disability meant that my motion below the waist was pretty compromised, as was my sensation. I was not able to feel things that happened below my hip bones the way that a non-disabled person could. I wondered if I would even be able to tell if a penis was in my vagina. And was my vagina supposed to do something once the penis was in it? Did other people's vaginas do something? Because mine seemed to just sit there.

These were pretty intimate questions, questions that I was too embarrassed to share with anyone, and that made me feel really anxious. I held a deep fear that maybe I wouldn't be able to have sex at all, that maybe I would fail at this act and that failure would leave me trapped in the most boring adulthood available. What if my vaginal (mis)behaviour confined me to live in a small town forever?! Considering that such an outcome seemed to me like a fate worse than death, I decided to face my fears and do it—I would try to fuck. The only way to get some answers was to risk it.

Enter Dan. He was my first real boyfriend. I set about dating him out of neither lust nor love, but rather my obsessive adulthood-attaining endeavour. He would be The One, I decided. He met all of my required credentials at the time. First, he was a boy. Second, he was my boyfriend. Third, he wanted to have sex with me. That was really all I needed. I was so determined to do it that I was not going to set the bar too high. And Dan was nice enough. He loved me, he had a truck, and he had really great hair. We talked on the phone after school every night and spent our lunch hours making out down by the quarry, just off school property. Our relationship felt like a perfect pathway to meeting my goals. After eight months of going steady, I decided it was time.

I undertook some initial preparations to ready myself. While for most of my peers this would have meant bashfully buying a box of condoms at the gas station in the next town over, my planning strategy was more involved. The first step was to develop a series of rigorous exercises that I would perform every night before falling asleep. I would lie in my bed and furtively contort my body into awkward poses I presumed were a crucial precursor to fucking. First, I would lift my butt high off the mattress, thrusting my pelvis into the air. In that half-raised state, I would then struggle to spread my legs as wide apart as possible, using my arms to shuffle my knees outward. Wary of the way that this stance created a triple chin, I would attempt to perform this feat while looking lascivious. My eyebrows would be provocatively arched. I would open my lips in a way that, I hoped, looked sensual. Should my ankles give out or my knees buckle, I would resolutely try again and again. I was a dedicated exerciser.

The second preparatory act was to enlist the help of a more experienced sex guide. Those deep questions—like what my vagina was supposed to do—were too tender to ask of anyone, but I felt I should at least seek out some more general advice. I enlisted Katherine for the job. Katherine was not only a good friend but also one of the most sexually active people I knew. Our teen years had looked very different. While I had passed my summers pumping gas at the local gas station (a.k.a. sitting on a lawn chair), she had spent all of hers away at summer camp. From June through July, Katherine's parents would send her off to different parts of the province, ostensibly to learn such skills as kayaking and wilderness training. Unbeknownst to them, Katherine would instead learn much more incendiary life lessons. She had come back from her various summer excursions with hickeys, nipple piercings, and sordid stories. Considering that thus far my forays around the bases had not gotten me much farther than first, I knew she could teach me a thing or two. We scheduled a Friday night "study session" to be held in the privacy of her bedroom.

Katherine had obviously done this before. I arrived at her house to find her prepared with plenty of fruit, which she had pilfered from her parents' kitchen: bananas, cucumbers, carrots, peaches, melons, and plums. She knew just which produce best suited sex tutorials.

The fruit, my anatomical guides, lay lined up across her black satin bedspread. I sat on the floor opposite the bed, ready to learn. This had been the bedroom where I had first gotten my period a year prior, where I had first kissed a boy, and where I had learned to put on makeup. Katherine's room had become the de facto location for rites of passage.

"Here," Katherine said, passing me a Smirnoff Ice cooler (her favourite drink).

I cracked open the bottle and gulped.

She stood beside the bed looking like a professional. A cigarette dangled from her hot pink lips, and her La Senza push-up miracle bra was achieving its desired effect. À la Britney Spears, the waist band of her thong peeked out above her low-rise jeans. With one hand on her hips, she launched into her lesson.

"You're not hopeless, but you do have a lot to learn," she began. "Let's start with this." She picked up the banana. "This is a dick." Next, she took a bite out of the plum, and with her mouth full, she held up the soft, exposed inner pulp and explained, "this is a vagina."

Katherine proved to be an immersive instructor. Her food-based lesson in human sexuality went on for well over an hour. She extrapolated on everything from how to properly shape one's lips around a banana/dick to how to avoid "pussy farts" (something I had never even heard of, let alone thought to avoid). I sat through it all enraptured, getting progressively drunk on Smirnoff coolers. Nearly everything that Katherine talked about was a revelation to me. By the time she was through, I was overwhelmed and even more scared. Learning that I knew nothing made sex seem all the more daunting.

But I could not back out now. Dan and I had set a date, and I was not going to cancel it. Everything was in place. His dad was going to be away for the weekend, and my parents believed I would be staying at a friend's. I had been practising my exercises for months, and I felt as physically ready as I'd ever be. Plus, Katherine had gifted me a congratulatory box of condoms. The time was now.

The following Friday night found me in Dan's bedroom. We sat facing each other on his bed. We were both naked except for our underwear: me in a sports bra and what I considered to be my sexiest pair of panties (pink with a cartoon cat on the front) and him in tattered boxer briefs. Neither one of us would look directly at the other. I focused my eyes on the glowing light of the candles I had spread around the room and tried to remember everything Katherine had taught me. Dan fiddled with the box of condoms, tossing it from one hand to the other.

"So, this is gonna be fun," he said, and nodded at me reassuringly.

"Uh, yeah," I said, frowning.

"You ready?" he asked.

"Yeah," I said and started kissing him.

Kissing was familiar. *I got this*, I thought. I began to calm down and hoped that everything would be totally intuitive. We made out for a while, our skinny arms fumbling around one another's skinny bodies, our hands hesitantly groping at each other. When I felt Dan's hard-on press up against my thigh, I pulled his boxers down like I knew what I was doing. My hands felt for his penis. I had always kept my eyes closed while kissing. But now I opened them, wanting to see it. I peeked down. I immediately stopped kissing him and pulled away. Dan's junk was much more intimidating than Katherine's banana had been.

"Don't be scared," Dan offered kindly. "Just pretend it's a Mars Bar."

I took a deep breath. And unfortunately, I took Dan's attempt at a reassuring metaphor literally. I bent down, put my mouth around his penis, and bit it. Perhaps it was the fact that my first sex tutorial had been entirely food-based. Or maybe it was the performance anxiety making me do strange things. Either way, when I began my first attempt at sex, I began it with my teeth. What I had hoped would be a preliminary blow job turned into a hard-earned lesson in What Not To Do. As my teeth sank into his skin, Dan yelped with fear and pain. I quickly unclenched my jaw and recoiled. We both jumped up, pulled our clothes on, and proceeded to not look directly at each other. I don't think we ever looked directly at each other again. We went to sleep that night without having sex and without ever really talking about it. We broke up a week later.

It follows that the remainder of my high school career remained predominantly sex-less. That fairly traumatizing experience with Dan kept me out of the saddle for quite a while. I did, however, eventually have penetrative sex, and when it happened, it happened without teeth or fanfare. In fact, it happened in exactly the way I could have predicted it would if I had not spent so much time worrying about it.

It was at a barn party celebrating our high school graduation. After enough drinks had been consumed, I unceremoniously angled myself into the backseat of my station wagon with a boy I had known since I was five. We proceeded to engage in the predictably uncomfortable paired aerobic activities that we classified as sex. It was unclear if my years of late-night exercises made the experience any better, or at the very least not totally terrible. Either way, in the end, the thing that I had spent so much time planning for lasted roughly five minutes and did absolutely nothing in the way of making me feel like a woman. It was remarkable only in that it was so unremarkable.

By the time I finally got around to having sex, I had already secured a scholarship to a far-off university. I had stopped thinking of sex as some sort of method for escaping my small town, and I was no longer as preoccupied with attaining adulthood. My disability-related worries notwithstanding, I fucked in my backseat that night just to prove to myself that I could. Knowing at least that much, I left town shortly thereafter and never moved back.

From rural Ontario, I resettled myself in Halifax, both to pursue post-secondary education and to continue my bumbling sexual development. My one-night stand—with a boy I had spent my childhood eating sand with—had not given me many reassurances. All I had learned about sex was to not bite a penis, but other than that I was uncertain about most everything. I knew I could at the very least do it in some capacity, but my anxieties persisted. The role of my vagina continued to be enigmatic. The type of mobility sex required was still an unknown variable. I still wanted answers. So I continued to try and seek them.

I met Matthew within two months of moving to Halifax. This was back when you could still smoke inside bars and you could easily doctor an ID. A well-placed drop of black nail polish bumped me up from eighteen to twenty-eight, and I slipped in and out of downtown bars unnoticed. Matthew and I met at a club called The Attic, previously known as My Apartment, later known as The Dome. He caught me as I stumbled around the dance floor in high-heeled boots I should never have tried to wear. I am hopeless in heels. Matthew grabbed my arm and rebalanced me as I tail-spinned out of an ungraceful dance manoeuvre. I looked up to thank him and saw that he was tall and handsome. Very, very tall, actually. So tall that I gave up trying to verbally communicate anything to him in the crowded bar. We wordlessly danced for a while, Matthew holding me as we swayed. At the end of the night, I gave him my number, feeling sheepish. Considering that all cultural commentary likens one's competency on the dance floor to their skills in the bedroom, I felt I had just given a rather unimpressive first impression. It was clear to Matthew that I could not cut a rug. If I couldn't dance, could I fuck? And would a very tall, handsome man even want to fuck me? My high school sexual history had not followed me across the country, but the damage it had done to my self-confidence had.

Luckily, Matthew could not tell from dancing with me that I had only had sex once in the back of my car for five minutes. He called me the next day, and we went on our first date shortly thereafter.

I would describe those preliminary dates if I could, but other than Matthew's towering height and incessant need to perform Dave Chappelle skits—he could gladly recite nearly the entire script of *Half Baked*—I can barely remember anything about our time together before "the incident."

It is entirely possible that I don't recall our first few chaste dates because they were mostly composed of me listening to the tired repetition of marijuana-related jokes. Needless to say, it wasn't love. But Matthew had other things I was interested in. Specifically, he was older than me and he had his own apartment. I believed that these credentials indicated that with Matthew I could experience the sophisticated, adult sex I had once imagined. I ambitiously hoped that with him I would figure out what sex was *really* meant to look like and whether or not I would be physically able to do it. Despite all of my sexual anxieties and past mortifications, I was still wildly curious, and I wasn't going to give up on fucking just yet.

It was our third or maybe our fourth date when he invited me over under the pretext of watching TV. Watching TV together is always a pretext. So we acted out each of those things that two people do while watching TV when they really just want to have sex: we sat too close together on the couch, our hands inched across the worn fabric towards one another, our arms wrapped around each other, and then eventually we were horizontal.

I knew right away that I had to pee. This is because a) as a general rule I always have to pee, and b) in situations that intimidate me that near-constant urge is multiplied by ten. It was no surprise when I felt that telltale tingle in my groin. Typically a part of being disabled for me is the constant responsibility of what the medical industry refers to as "bladder management." What this means: my bladder, unlike the bladder of some others, does its own thing, and all I have to do is manage it. It pees when it wants to, whether or not I have signalled that it is an appropriate time to let loose. In the past it decided to empty itself while I was talking to my first big crush, while I was kayaking in the ocean, and while I was on an airplane, stuck in my seat during takeoff. Having such a domineering bladder is pretty inconvenient, and so to better control it, I starve it. Liquid intake is kept to a minimum before and during dates, movies, plane rides, and any other situation where toilets are not at the ready. Catheterization[6] must also happen pretty often, just to make sure that my bladder is sufficiently empty and cannot surprise attack my jeans (and my sense of pride) at inopportune moments. All this to say that I should have been much more attentive to the tingle.

But I wasn't. I just did not want to be. At the age of eighteen, I was still painfully aware of the ways in which I wasn't "normal." My overactive bladder was very far from normal. I had been counting, and I had already excused myself and run to the bathroom three times by this point. I felt that this number of bathroom breaks was clearly bizarre. I was sure that this more experienced older man would be completely turned off by my excessive bodily functions. I was even willing to bet that one more pee break would end this date and cancel the sweet sex I was expecting. My only option: hold it.

---

6 Catheterization is something that a lot of people do. A catheter is a clear, plastic tube-y thing that is inserted into the urethra and reaches up into the bladder. Some people have a catheter inserted all the time, while others, like myself, do intermittent self-catheterization. This means that when I feel the need to pee, I stick the tube-y thing into my urethra and pee comes out. I use a 14 French catheter, which you don't really need to know, but it sounds kind of sexy.

We moved off the couch and progressed into his bedroom. All the while my knees were shaking with the effort to control my bladder. He pressed me up against the wall and kissed my neck. It may have felt good, but I was too distracted to notice. My shirt came off and then his belt. He threw me on the bed. We continued to undress each other. I continued to hold my pee. Soon, he was just in his boxer shorts and black dress socks and I was in nearly nothing. I lay sprawled out on the bed and considered getting up to go to the bathroom. But I couldn't do it! I was too embarrassed! And that's when it happened. Matthew, being completely unaware of my inner turmoil, seductively reached his hand down and slipped it underneath the soft cotton of my underwear. My cunt felt wet and ready. And so did my thighs. And quickly his fingers felt strangely wet as well. It became immediately obvious to both of us that this warmth spreading over us was not vaginal lubrication, but was instead a steady stream of urine, wetting my body and his, plus his expensive Egyptian cotton sheets and his $800 queen-sized mattress. I was pissing everywhere. I lay in my self-made yellow pool for half a second and determined that there was no way to recover from this. I stood up, muttered an apology, pulled my jeans on over my damp legs, and fled.

Matthew called me for weeks afterward. He would leave reassuring messages on my answering machine, telling me not to worry and asking me to call him back. I never did.

I wish I could say that this was it, that this was the entirety of my fumbles, bumbles, and flounders as I have stepped ungracefully into my sexuality. But in actual fact I could go on and on, seemingly without end. Sex has never come easily to me. It has not been intuitive, natural, or graceful. It has been hilarious, thought-provoking, and full of hard lessons, but it has never looked the way that I thought it was supposed to.

Why have I found myself in these situations? It's not because I am not good at this kind of thing, nor is it a result of my disability. As it turned out, my teenage worries were misplaced, and it proved untrue that being disabled would make sex difficult for me. No, I have experienced these mishaps because, like so many of us, I was largely misinformed about the nature of sex. I was misled to believe that there was some kind of formula, a trajectory we are all supposed to know and to follow. I naively took the images of sex taught to me by movies, TV, and porn as truth. I believed that I was supposed to move seamlessly from being clothed to being penetrated, that it would always result in simultaneous orgasms, and that I would always enjoy it. Without any sort of sex education (notwithstanding Katherine and her melons) or a space where I could ask difficult and vulnerable questions, I was left to make false assumptions. And so it is only through experience that I have come to realize that there is in fact no specific procedure, no right way of doing it. I know now that sex can look a million and one different ways. Luckily, I have discovered that I do not have to fit my disabled body into an able-bodied portrait of erotic intimacy. I can create my own framework and choose my own desires.

I think that, for many of us, the sex we are having does not match our idea of what sex is supposed to be. With so much shame and silence around sex, our imaginations are unrealistic, informed as they are by unattainable standards and glaring absences in sexual health education. As I've found out, sex can be uncomfortable and clunky and vulnerable. We all sometimes pee and bite and fart when we don't mean to. Which is exactly why I do the work that I do. I might have saved years of confusion if I'd had access to someone to talk to about bodily mechanics. And my own early sex life would have been vastly different if I'd had other disabled, sexual people as role models. But I didn't.

So here I am now, truthfully and shamelessly telling you this:

I have mistakenly tried to eat a penis.
I have accidentally peed on an adult man.
I have farted, loudly, right in that beautiful moment of orgasm.
I have said the wrong thing at absolutely every chance.
I have giggled instead of groaned,
have gagged instead of gushed.
I would prefer to be honest. May all my inexpert errors reassure you: you are not alone.

Fresh-Faced and Orgasm Free

I woke up this morning and got myself off. It is an exercise I have been trying to incorporate more and more into my daily life. Some people take up meditation, others cut out gluten. But to me increased masturbation seems like the ticket to a happier, healthier, and less stressful life. I am writing this in the grey days of January, when the new year is affording us some hopeful vigour despite the fact that winter is only just getting its footing. The ambition of our collective resolutions is in the air, and I am taking it all to heart, or rather to my clit. I have seven sex toys lined up beside my bed along with a bottle of lube. Multi-coloured and pretty, the toys stand at attention, offering me promises of pleasure. I have been making sure that at least four times a week, I begin my day by reaching out to them. It would be quicker not to. My days are full, and the most practical way to start them would probably be with coffee and typing. But getting up for the immediate click-click-click of fingers on keys proves depressing. I do it, but I don't like it. And so, instead, I treat myself to these four mornings with another kind of device. I am not quick. I have never been quick. These morning masturbations are drawn out. I need at least forty-five minutes to reach my climactic end goal, and that is with my vibrators. Those people who can rub one out in the bathroom stall on their lunch break—that has never been me. When I'm fucking myself, it is a lengthy endeavour. I've been practising for years, and still my body remains resistant to my fingers, demanding substantial time and attention before being charmed. I've accepted it. I'm just not easy.

It has always been this way for me. I did not begin my work at a sex shop as an orgasm aficionado. As indicated by my aforementioned cringeworthy exploits, I did not always play well with others. Unfortunately, I was not so skilled at playing with myself either. At the time that I was hired by Venus Envy—the sex shop where I now work— I had experienced roughly two orgasms in my entire life (one from a man named Thor, which is a whole other story, and one by my own hand, after about an hour of strenuous digital explorations).

I got the job at Venus Envy the summer I turned twenty-three. I had just graduated with a liberal arts degree, and I was looking for absolutely any sort of work I could find. I had papered the town with résumés and had only gotten two call-backs. Coincidentally they were both for jobs at high-end, tourist-driven candy shops, neither of which hired me. Apparently I hadn't had enough "experience with candy." My options were seeming pretty bleak when Venus Envy called me in for an interview. I was terrified.

I had applied at the store with absolutely no expectations. Venus Envy is an award-winning, education-based sex shop, a pillar of Halifax's queer community, and the only place of its kind east of Toronto. Considering it has such credentials, I assumed the staff were required to come armed with a few impressive qualifications of their own, none of which I had. I lacked a background in sexual health; I did not identify as queer (yet); and I had not had a single moment of purely enjoyable, uncomplicated sex. It appeared as though the odds were against me. Yet I applied all the same. It seemed like a dream job and I had to try.

Here I must confess: I was not initially so wildly interested in working at a sex shop because I cared a lot about sex. At this point in my life, I had stopped even thinking about it much. My attempts at doing it (both alone and with others) having largely failed me, any feelings of lust I had previously had were now mostly in remission. Sex was not the driving force behind my bold job application. The truth is, I was most interested in the books. Venus Envy has the very best books. Pages and pages of new fiction, feminist publications, and cultural critiques line the walls of the store. I wanted to dive into all of them. I wanted to get lost in Venus Envy's literature, to take each shiny new paperback home and make it my own. Working there seemed to be the best way to make this happen. I was in it for the books, not the dildos. And I really wanted in.

I went to the interview dressed in my most professional-looking outfit. I also pre-emptively constructed anecdotes that I hoped would make me appear mature, confident, and sexually experienced. I had even gone so far as to study some anatomical diagrams online the night before, in case the interview had a pop-quiz component. I furtively reviewed the names of all the parts, mouthing the words "labia majora," "pubic mound," and "frenulum," in my bedroom while my roommates watched the baseball game on TV just outside the door.

It turned out that all my efforts had been in vain. The interview was easy. I did not have to reference my sexual history nor answer any multiple-choice questions. My orientation and prowess, or lack thereof, were irrelevant. I was only required to chat with my soon-to-be-boss. We talked mostly about my retail experience and whether or not I liked doing things like dusting and reshelving stock. It was all pretty straightforward, and I felt confident I had come off appearing pretty normal, perhaps even capable and charming. I had. I got the job and started work a week later.

I loved it immediately. It felt perfect for me from the very start. Talking about sex came easily. Someone would walk in and uncomfortably browse the shelves for forty-five minutes before timidly admitting that they wanted to purchase their first sex toy. Or someone would saunter in nonchalantly and tell me that they needed a bigger butt plug. Groups of teenagers, older lovers, queer couples, baffled husbands, mothers and daughters—they all came in, feeling anxious or at home or sometimes unaware of what they were walking into. I loved helping all of them.

Working at a sex shop is all about hearing secrets and holding truths, about trying to alleviate weight from people's shoulders and shame from people's chests. It felt like an honour to be doing it. And despite my own orgasmic difficulties and lack of sexual experience, I was good at it. I was a good listener. And providing advice and information that could mitigate someone's fears or fulfill their desires was simple. I just had to repeat all that I had been taught in my training and mimic the vernacular of my co-workers.

"This toy is made of 100% medical-grade silicone, which is great, because it means it can be sterilized."

"This toy is well-shaped for external stimulation. The clitoris has eight thousand nerve endings, which means that vibrations can feel really awesome, or, of course, not awesome at all, because all bodies are different."

"When buying your first butt plug, you should start small, make sure your toy has a base, and always add a lot of lube."

It was all a matter of repetition and friendly delivery. For the first few months it felt easy. People would ask questions, and I would listen attentively and then recite a response. No problem. Until one day it stopped being easy. And then everything felt like a problem.

It was about my sixth month into it. I had been working at the shop for long enough to begin feeling totally comfortable there. The job was as dreamy as I had imagined it would be: I was allowed to borrow whichever books I wanted and even read them in the shop if there were no customers around. I was eating words for breakfast, consuming feminist theory at a rapid pace. I was all alone in the shop and immersed in a queer fiction novel when the customer walked in.

They looked about my age, maybe a few years younger. Blonde hair spilled asymmetrically around their face, and an old backpack, held together with patches, was slung across their shoulders. They entered the store and immediately ducked behind a bookshelf without looking up. From where I was standing, I could see that they were chewing the skin around their thumb and closely examining the toe of their left boot rather than the books on the shelf in front of them. These were all the telltale signs of a nervous customer, and so I allowed them their space.[7]

For half an hour I puttered around them while they lifted boxes of tampons, examined bottles of lube, and

---

7 It should be noted that this customer is a construction. Staying true to the Unofficial Pact of Sex Shop Workers, I would never, ever, disclose information about any person who came into the store. This nervous customer is a made-up version of someone who could be real, and this experience is an exaggerated account of some things that could happen.

put each item back down before stuffing their hands hard into their pockets. I said hello at one point, but they ignored me, or maybe didn't hear me. As they continued their meandering explorations of the shop, they moved closer and closer to the back wall. The back wall is a site of anxiety for many people. Dozens of sex toys lean upright on their shelves. Above the vibrators hang tough-looking black leather harnesses. From one corner protrude twenty dildos with names like Outlaw, Tsunami, and Buck. While we try to make the space as welcoming as we can, given the titillating nature of sex toys, it is difficult to mediate some people's reactions. A lot of folks respond to a wall of dildos by immediately grabbing a cock and engaging their friends in a dildo sword fight. Others, like this person, seem not to want to be near it. I am more partial to the timid kind of customer myself. As someone who has also been daunted by sex, this is the kind of customer I can most relate to.

They finally reached the rear of the shop and stood in front of the vibrating bullets with their arms crossed tightly over their chest. I approached them.

"Do you need help finding anything today?" I asked, trying to sound especially congenial. They shook their head without looking at me.

"Okay, cool," I continued with a chipper voice. "Well, these toys all have batteries in them so you can feel them in your hands if that's helpf—"

The customer's confession exploded from their mouth and cut me off. Their words were rushed and jumbled.

"I can't orgasm. I have been trying my whole life, and I've just never done it. My friends say they do it all the time, and they think I'm a weirdo. They even squirt! I

must be like, broken down there or something, right?"
They gestured downward.

Their face was pale, and they seemed so worried that I
immediately empathized. I knew this feeling. And I believed I knew how to reassure this person, having heard my
co-workers address concerns like this many times before. I
started into a comforting spiel, offering generic pieces of
advice and platitudes. I talked about how all bodies are different, how we all need different lengths of time, different
pressure, different toys, and different types of stimulation.

Comforted, the customer tentatively looked at toys with
me. After we selected one, we moved on to books, and I
pointed out some helpful orgasm guides that my co-workers had told me were the most informative. Lastly, we chose
a bottle of lube to accompany the vibrator. As we selected
items, I watched the customer's shoulders move away from
their ears and saw their face open up.

It was as we were finishing up, while I swiped the debit card
and bagged the items, that the customer asked me the most
difficult question: "So these things worked for you, right?"

I had never been asked this before. A skill you learn when
working in a sex shop is to deflect attention away from yourself. You are only an anonymous sounding board for other
people's personal narratives. My sexual experiences and
preferences had never been dragged into the mix.

I am a terrible liar, and the truth was that these things had
not worked for me. I had not even tried to make anything
work for me. I had been employed at Venus Envy for half
a year and I had been spending all of my paycheques on
books. My library had evolved, but my capacity to experience pleasure had remained stagnant. I had not even really
been thinking about sex at all. Absurd, I know, consider-

ing I was talking about it every day. But I was never talking about *my* sex; I was only listening to the sex stories of others. I was learning how to be a good listener, not a good lover. I had perhaps even subconsciously been avoiding reflecting on my own sex life, disappointing as it had been. When you spend all day talking to people who are doing some sort of fucking, it can be depressing to remember that you are not. But now I was being directly asked about it, and there was nothing I could do but lie.

"Yeah, uh, definitely. Definitely did. These are some great, uh, great things ya got here. Great stuff."

When the customer left, I sat down, floored by the full-on recognition that I still knew nothing about coming from a personal standpoint. For months now, I had been talking about the practicalities of sexual satisfaction, waxing poetic on sex toys as if I knew their value. But all I was doing was regurgitating rather than speaking from any actual experience. On the plus side, I no longer wasted much time worrying about sex. I had stopped actively examining all of my long-standing sex-related neuroses. But this was not because I had worked through them. I had simply stuffed all of my concerns under the rug. The bulging bulk of them was suddenly apparent.

Since starting work at Venus Envy, I had not masturbated, had not orgasmed, and had not used the one single vibrator I had ambitiously purchased on my first day of work. The pink, jelly, phallic object had been lying fallow in my underwear drawer for months now. There would be times, I realized, when having actually done something myself would make it much easier to talk about that thing. Being able to give myself an orgasm seemed a suitable preliminary skill to have.

It was not as though I had never tried to fwap one out

before. I had thoroughly examined my stuff below the belt and had found it (sort of) fun on (just) one occasion. But for the most part, my explorations of my Southern Hemisphere had found more valleys than peaks. No matter how hard I pressed, how long I rubbed, whether I up-stroked, down-stroked or kept it a little to the left, almost all of my results had been anticlimactic. I was not sure what I was doing wrong, but clearly something was not right.

It could be that I was disabled. Just as I had worried that a spinal cord injury would keep me from knowing how to fuck others, I also worried that it would keep me from feeling good on my own. Since the accident I had been back and forth from doctor to doctor many, many times. At each examination I had been subjected to enough tests with the Wartenberg wheel to know that my sensation was limited. With my eyes closed, the doctors would prick my legs with needles, press hot and cold objects to my toes, and roll the wheel along my skin. Their touches would resonate as ghostly tingles. I knew something was there, but I did not know exactly what. The doctors would peer down over their noses at me lying prostrate on the white, papered examination table and label me a "four out of five." They would send me home without explaining what that meant. I knew not to test water temperature with my toes, but I imagined it all must have some larger-scale consequences than an inability to determine the tepidness of pool water with my feet. Perhaps part of the repercussions was that those eight thousand nerve endings in my clit were not operating to their full capacity? Maybe my so-called "magic button" was not so magic after all? Maybe this was why I had never really gotten all hot and bothered from touching it?

Or maybe the problem was simply a lack of imagination. I had learned my vulva through the least sexy framework possible: the medical lens. I had sustained my spinal cord injury at the green age of nine. This meant that I quite quickly learned all about my body as though it were a problem, something that I had to learn to work with and rehabilitate. I grew to know my junk as something that would leak urine and that I had to take care of by frequently catheterizing. I learned all about my urethral opening and how to insert a lubricated plastic tube into it long before I knew what the clitoris was or what sorts of things could feel good in other holes. My vulva was simply another part of my disability, and it was a place I knew intimately in that context. Every time I went to the bathroom, I would gently spread open my labia to insert the catheter. Touching myself was so common that it was hard to imagine it as a sexual experience. It was functional, not hot. Necessary, not fun. Maybe it was this long-standing pattern that was holding me back, and to get the goods out of masturbating, I had to work on some reprogramming? Could that have been my wrong turn?

Regardless of what the root problem was, the outcome had been that I had, at some point, accepted that I was one of those women who "just couldn't." But my experience with the customer had called this thesis into question. I decided to extend the kind reassurances I issued to others to myself as well. I was ready to revisit my cunt. And predictably, I decided to begin with books.

I diligently brought home a copy of every orgasm book in the shop. Beginning with *The Elusive Orgasm* and moving all the way through to *Slow Sex*, I searched the pages. For weeks, the stack sat beside my bed and I plowed through it every night. I dog-eared pages and highlighted pointers. I was an industrious scientist, a dedicated student. I was trying to somehow draw out a map of what I should do to successfully come.

I was looking specifically for experiences like mine, for heartening anecdotes and some validation. I suppose what I needed was something like *Chicken Soup for the Vulva*. Instead, I discovered some really helpful information, but also some questionable constructs. While it was great to read about anatomy and technique, something in these pages was not resonating with me.

In some books, the problem was the oft-repeated sentiment that you would "just know." This indefinite stock phrase was so lacking that it felt more like a misdirection than a guide post. If one is in search of something hard to find, it doesn't help to tell them to just follow their intuition. Instead, they need some clear markers that they are on the right path. Telling everyone that they would all "just know" implies that all orgasms feel the same for all people. Orgasms always feel like something so indefinable they can't be described?! I didn't buy it. If it was true that everyone liked different kinds of sex (and my work at the shop had definitely affirmed this truth) then it must also follow that everyone experiences orgasms differently. I resented the amorphous homogeny that so many of these orgasm guides were putting forth.

In other texts, the obvious problem was the focus put on partnered sex and penetration. I had stopped trying to find my sweet spot at someone else's hand long ago. I knew from experience that having somebody or something inside of me was not a sure way to success, so I immediately disregarded any advice that indicated having my partner's penis in my vagina was going to be the thing. My orgasm would not be codependent.

But there was something more to it than these simple shortcomings. Something else was not fitting quite right; there was some sort of larger structural issue at play. It took me a while, but eventually I was able to pinpoint it. The problem was that none of this stuff made room for my disability. Every sex expert, masturbating master, and intimacy theorist whose writing I was reading was operating under the assumption that I was able-bodied.

"Simply move your fingers in rapid, circular motions around the clitoris," the author would write, presuming that moving one's fingers was always "simple."

"The clitoris will swell and protrude when stimulated." These accounts didn't take into consideration that perhaps not every clitoris was necessarily capable of swelling.

"You should feel your vagina contract," stated one book. But could my vagina contract? What muscles made it contract? Could those muscles be affected by my disability? And what would those contractions feel like?

The assumption of able-bodiedness meant that almost all of the informative orgasm guides I was reading left me with more questions. None of these books were speaking to my experience. It occurred to me that perhaps I had yet to learn my way of coming because all the step-by-step methods I was reading, all the porn I had watched, and all the sex I had had thus far had not considered my disability. Everything I had read, watched, and done had been about being able-bodied, something I was just not and did not want to be.

It reminded me of the way I had been taught to stand up out of a chair. All the doctors and rehabilitation experts would tell me not to use my strong arms to pull myself upright. They would encourage me to practise engaging my core, to use my quads, to rely on my ankles. This was the "correct" way of standing up. But the abilities of my core, quads, and ankles have always been dubious—they are not my strongest assets—while my biceps have always been highly over-developed. I had long ago stopped listening to all the specialists. I was very happy using my arms to pull myself up off the couch or the kitchen chair. When they all described to me the "correct" way of doing something, they were using "correct" as synonymous with "able-bodied." But my disabled way of moving worked just fine for me, and I was not interested in rehabilitating myself so that I could better conform to a normative way of being. I loved my difference. I believed—still believe—that the most beautiful part of residing in difference is that you get to reconstruct everything we are told is truth and build for yourself a way of being that fits for you. The way I stand up with my arms is fabulous, the way I carry things in my teeth rather than my hands is magnificent, and the way I drag my right foot is spectacular. Each of those movements collide and create a way of moving through the world that is the most efficient for me. I had learned to disregard therapists who had tried to correct me and ignore anyone who described a "proper" way of doing something.

I decided to apply this attitude to fucking myself. It was such a relief to realize that just as there isn't one right way to get up and down the stairs, there isn't one right way to get off. I approached my newfound masturbatory practice with this as my mantra. Realizing that none of the paths had been constructed in my favour freed me to bushwhack my own path and follow my own particular swaying way to my destination. My jerk-off practice was a deconstruction site. I was reworking everything.

I went home from work each night and practised. My self-love sessions were long-winded, to say the least. With absolutely every part and position now becoming a potential pleasure zone, the variables I could try were endless. I put toys in all new places. Nothing was off limits. I worked my way through bottles and bottles of lube and brought home a plethora of new toys. My bedside table was no longer laden with books but with butt plugs (and dildos and nipple clamps and vibrators). I was willing to try everything and anything in the name of arriving at my pleasure. And the best part about all of this was that my new efforts were not being undertaken out of fear, anxiety, or a pressure to be "normal." Instead, my bodily explorations, now unencumbered from an ill-fitting and able-bodied standard, held the potential for all sorts of magic.

I developed my desires and the shape of my sex in that way, on my own terms. I did not follow others' advice but created my own strategy. And it did not happen "just like that." I cannot write that one night my clandestine attempts at coming bore fruit and I was ushered into the secret society of Women Who Come. It would perhaps be easier to write that I eventually put all the right things in all the right spots, and there it was, just like that—I "just knew."

But that would be completely untrue. Of course it did not work that way. All my late-night loving taught me a lot, but it didn't teach me to be a sure thing. I still need to be wooed. I still have to practise four times a week. I cannot just roll over and get myself off in a hot minute before I enter into my day. And then when I do come, I do not know exactly if it feels like it is supposed to feel. I do not know if it feels the way yours feels. I am willing to bet we all orgasm differently, considering we all have different parts. My coming is all my own. My orgasms are unpredictable and hard to define. They are not marked off or delineated. Instead, my body tumbles in and out of feeling good, just as it tumbles in and out of being upright. I trip into coming.

So, I woke up this morning and got myself off. Today it took roughly forty-five minutes, and I did it exactly the way I wanted to.

The Lady & The Butch

I heard the tell-tale *ding dong* of the shop's door and looked up. I had been absorbed in my book, the store having been empty for the last hour and a half. It was one of those wet, grey days that are so painfully commonplace in Halifax. The damp cold will seep into your bones, securing itself inside your very core for the duration of the winter. Nobody was going to leave their house and come to a sex shop that afternoon. I was willing to bet that no one was even having sex, anywhere, in the entire city. We were all too depressed as a population, oppressed as we were beneath the low-slung metallic sky. So, I gave myself to the pages of books, certain that I had the day to myself.

Two people entered into the warmth of the shop, and my surprise deepened. They seemed like an unlikely pair to be coming into a sex shop together. The taller person brought up the rear, squeezing their broad shoulders through the door. I noticed them first, admittedly not because of their height but because they were a stone-cold fox. Their hair, cut short against their scalp, seemed to have partially frozen in the winter's air, some strands turned icy silver amongst the dark crop. They were wearing a Carhartt suit, faded brown with a zipper up the front and dirt rubbed deep into the knees. Their hands were big and bare, turned red from the chill and tightly curled around the back handles of a wheelchair. They pushed the chair forward with a confident strut, a swagger often attributed to butches of a certain generation. The other person led the way in their chair. This person was older—I would have guessed somewhere in their eighties or early nineties. Their skin had that translucence associated with old age, veins appearing as bulging rivers on their skin's pale surface. This person was quite small, and they seemed delicate and fragile. Most of their body was protectively enclosed in a purple, floral-print, one-piece snow suit. Topping all of this was a tightly curled crown of hair which had been dyed a shade of mauve, perfectly complementing the suit.

Despite the older person's small stature and presumed fragility, I could hear them assuredly barking orders at the person they were with, their voice shaped by that particular rasp induced by years of cigarette smoking. "Move me in here faster! I am nearly dead from all this goddamn fucking cold, Janet!" They declared, as the other person, whom I now knew to be Janet, pushed them inside. This litany of complaints continued as the two slowly approached the counter. Janet, for their part, continued to say nothing.

I put my book down and smiled, prepared to help the pair, but also already feeling a little fearful of this brash and seemingly tough-as-fuck elderly person. I felt certain I could not be subjected to such stern commands and maintain as confident a strut and posture as Janet.

The two reached me, and with eyes level to the counter, the older one glared at me. My saccharine smile was not fooling anyone. This person could smell my hesitation. They looked me up and down.

"Well, tell her, Janet," the purple-clad person ordered. I turned my eyes up to Janet. This person also seemed to be able to read me, which was embarrassing because I was entertaining some pretty dirty thoughts about them. Janet cocked their eyebrow, smirked, and reached into the front pocket of the faded work suit. They pulled out a credit card and threw it down on the counter.

"Get this woman whatever she wants. Price don't matter."

The directions were clear and clipped, as though Janet would prefer not to speak at all.

I nodded obediently and then turned my gaze to the older woman. She stared at me with menace in her eyes, daring me to try and talk to her about sex.

I shifted my focus again, intending to issue a pleading stare toward Janet, but they were already sauntering to the door, their broad back to me. Appearing to sense my doubt, Janet turned and came back to us.

"My number," they said, laying a post-it on the counter with seven digits scrawled messily across it. I blushed and then gave a knowing smirk of my own.

"To call me. When she's through. So I can pick her up," Janet finished. I blushed redder, swallowed the smirk off my now-sheepish face, and nodded.

Janet left, squeezing through the door. I turned to the older woman. Her arms were folded across her small chest, and she looked a little like a withered concord grape, sour through and through. I almost laughed.

"She's my granddaughter-in-law. She's one of those lesbians," she rasped. I nodded. I had been exclusively bobbing my head since this duo had come in, feeling unsure of my ability to form any sort of coherent sentence. My neck was feeling tired.

"Are you a queer? You sure don't look like much of one," she asked. I mean, I suppose she was asking a question, but it felt more like a back-handed compliment, an approval of what she was reading as my normative femininity. And this could have been a moment where I leaned into femme invisibility and didn't divulge much, driven as I was to avoid this granny's ridicule. But that would have been dishonest. So, I nodded again.

"Hmmm," she grunted. And then she surprised me by saying, "Good. I prefer that. My granddaughter is a queer lesbian, and she knows all about sex. Lesbians always do, you see. It is their specialty," she continued, "or so I am told. Me, I'm definitely not one of 'em. I was married to the same man for forty-six years. My Darrel. He died twenty-three years ago and I haven't let no hand touch me since. Not even my own. Thought it would be unfaithful."

At this point her eyes welled up. I could see a crack in her purpled, hardened front. I went to reach my hand out to hers, covered in age spots and clasped on the countertop, but before I could interject with a touch or some sort of re-assurance, she pulled her hands back and continued.

For twenty minutes, she told me all about Darrel, his work as a mechanic, his love of dogs, her love of him, and the babies they raised together. It was one long, linear narrative, full of the most caring details and all delivered in her contrary bark of a voice. It was as if prefacing her purchase with the story of her loved one would soothe her guilt, would cancel out the infidelity she believed she may be perpetrating. Eventually she concluded with her reason for being here in front of me.

"So now Susanne, my granddaughter, Ronny's eldest, and Janet there, her wife, say I need to buy a dildo. They know all about them, you see, because they are queer lesbi-ans. They say if I just have some fun and let loose a little for a minute, I won't be so cranky all the time. Sus even thinks it'll help with my arthritis, but to that I say she's one of those woo-woo hippie weirdos who don't know a goddamn thing. Anyway, here I am, I suppose, and you better fix me up." It was an order, one I was sure I could fill.

There are moments when this work is intimidating. There can be such profound vulnerability in sharing a sexual history, a long-held desire, or an unexpressed fear. In my own moments of uncertainty, I find myself wanting to have a "right answer," to be able to sell something or say something that will cure all. There is no right answer or perfect sex toy. The best we can do is witness one another in these exchanges. To see one another as whole and human, to treat each other with compassion. I did not possess the magic cure to assure this grandmother that she could have a sexual self that existed outside of her marriage. But I could take her in, in her entirety, learn her history and her wants, and carry that as she chose to try something new.

The woman and I walked over to the wall of sex toys, all of them charged and lined up for her to inspect. We perused vibrators, dildos, nipple clamps, and cock rings. She held the vibrators in her hands, laughing a hoarse yap as they buzzed against her fingertips. She asked me the standard questions: Which one is the best one? Which one do you like? Do women really buy these things? I answered each to the best of my ability and eventually she settled on a cute battery-powered vibe in her favourite colour (purple).

Back at the counter, I rang her through. I put batteries in her toy and made sure it all worked so that it would be ready to go when she got home. I gave her an information sheet, telling her all about cleaning it. I reassured her that her purchase was entirely normal and very classy and she just might like it. Then I called Janet to let her know we were all finished up.

As we waited for her ride, I tried to make small talk with the older woman, but she was strangely quiet, looking down rather than glaring at me with those penetrating blue eyes. I thought perhaps she was embarrassed, having just revealed to me some of her more intimate secrets. But then she said, "let me see that."

I realized she had not been looking down bashfully, but had been intently examining the pride jewellery displayed in the front of our counter. I lifted the glass top and she reached in, pulling a beaded rainbow necklace in between her crooked fingers.

"This is for the gays, right?" she asked me.

"Yeah, the rainbow is a symbol of gay pride."

"I'll take one of these then," she said.

I pulled the rainbow choker out of the case and clasped it around her neck. Janet walked in just as I was holding up a mirror, showing the grandmother how perfectly suited the beads were to her snow suit.

The two smiled at each other.

"What took you so long, Janet?! I'm nearly dead from how goddamn hot it is in here! Leaving me all alone with a bunch of queer lesbians! You would!"

Janet smiled and almost chortled, obviously impervious to the grandmother's near constant string of complaints and reprimands. They left together, moving as a single unit back out into the cold.

The next week we got a phone call down at the shop. It was my day off, so my co-worker took it. She said an older woman with a raspy voice had called looking for the blonde queer lesbian. She wanted to tell me thank you, and that it was a good choice even though her arthritis was still aching.

Disabled Dyke on a Trike

Halifax is a city with hills. On bike rides, I career down them, helmet off, trying to attain lightning speed. Or I crawl up them, slow but sure, breathing heavily. I live on the steepest hill of them all, right at the bottom. This makes my bike rides home most satisfying. On the last leg of my journey, I don't need to pedal at all. I hold my legs out as I am propelled down, down, *down* to my front door, the world a blur of coloured clapboard at my sides and a shining ocean ahead of me. Going up the hill on my way to work is more difficult. I push my bike up, up, *up*, using my whole body to move its weight.

My bike is heavy. It's really more of a tricycle, a big red bike with "training wheels" attached on the back. I use quotations because they look like training wheels, but they are not. I am not training for anything. They will never be removed, forever there to support me, balancing me as I move through the city. I am not, and never will be, stable enough to maneuver a bike on two wheels. The idea of even sitting on one, feet placed on pedals so far from the ground, makes me nervous. My weight would shift hopelessly back and forth. I would be flat on the pavement in one fell swoop.

My body is just not balanced. Instead, it is one beautiful, chaotic mess. Above the waist, I can manipulate my shoulders, arms, hands, and fingers with ease. I can turn my neck from left to right and cock my head at will. I can whisper sweet nothings or scream loud somethings at absolutely any time I want to. The top half of my body is at my mind's command. It is below the waist that things get more complicated. The messages moving through my spinal cord to my lower body get jumbled up and misshapen, making my movements jolted. The idea of walking that I hold in my head gets lost in translation, and my legs scissor in and out. My hips sway back and forth. My toes drag slowly against the ground. It is not balanced. What comes out is a way of moving my body that is subject to trips, falls, and unpredictable veers. But what I lack in balance, I make up for in grace. These differences are not to be pitied and definitely not to be "righted." They are completely correct, in all of their disarray. They may disallow me from riding a two-wheeled bike, but the bike I have now is more perfect than anything I could have imagined.

My bike was built for me by a boy named Bobby, who I thought I was in love with one summer. I spent August nights at his house, and in the mornings, he would watch me pedal away awkwardly on a bike I had inherited from my grandfather, a bike built for the elderly, to be maneuvered through the flat lanes of Florida's trailer park retirement communities. The seat was huge, made for a butt at least five times wider than mine, and surrounded by three equally large wheels, one out front and two in the back. It weighed a tonne, took corners at dangerously teetering angles, and forced me to move at a crawl no matter how hard I pedalled.

As a bike mechanic, Bobby took it upon himself to build me something better. It took him a few months to complete his project, and he surprised me with the new bike right before the winter set in. It was incredible. Bright red and light-weight. I fell in love with it immediately. The small wheels he had attached on the back of a typical, two-wheeled road bike were light but still strong enough to keep me balanced. Affixed to the bike by springs, they cornered smoothly and sturdily. I could move much faster up and down hills, around bends and over speed bumps. I felt powerful, freed, and newly mobile in a way that only those who have had their mobility compromised can truly understand. To be able to cross distances and get to places that I could never have reached before—it was a dream. But, even so, there was a moment of uncertainty.

My initial response upon receiving the gift was an old, familiar shame. Bobby looked at me, proud of what he had built. I looked at the bike and wondered what people would think when they saw an adult careening through town on training wheels. No stranger to being stared at, I imagined the impact this unusual bike could have on onlookers, the questions it would garner, the gesticulations from strangers. Bobby looked to me; I looked to the bike. I considered the bike and chose it, an act of choosing myself.

It's four years later, and I'm still in love with my bike. I am still pushing it up hills and propelling it down them, biking to and from work, going back and forth from dinner parties to dance parties. It's not always easy. My training wheels shield my skin from scrapes against cement, but do nothing to protect against social commentary. The adage about sticks and stones doesn't hold water. Words *do* hurt.

It was a sunny Sunday morning, and I was biking to a breakfast date. I had spent the morning in bed with my girlfriend, and as I biked uphill, I felt confident and sexy.

The incline was slight, but I was still moving slowly and working hard, my body shifting from side to side. The street was closed to traffic due to a marathon running through the centre of town, and the empty expanse felt free and open, just for me. I was getting into a flow, pedals rotating smoothly, when I heard the snickers. There were three men to my right, sitting on their stoop in the morning sunshine. I turned to them as one said, "Isn't it time to take off your training wheels?" I almost stopped. A part of me wanted to offer an explanation for my body, to make myself legible. But as the men stared blankly back at me, I decided they were not worth the time. I was late for breakfast, and I was hungry. As I biked on, I heard them laughing at my back. One of the men said, "Look at the way she's moving." Then, I thought I heard another use the word "retard." I looked back to see them mimicking my body's movements, rendering my adaptations into points of weakness.

Comments about my bike are not rare, and my initial concerns about people's reactions to it were correct: people *do* think that a grown woman with training wheels is a sight to be mocked. The general public *does* believe that my brazen display of difference leaves me open to their criticisms. It *is* as though I am asking for it, that the more space my disabled body takes up, the more others are compelled to reduce it into something they can minimize.

Shouts and mutters of this sort have happened to me so often that I have developed different protections against them. Sometimes I use a thick skin and a short-term memory approach—I try to let ableist slurs ricochet off of me and arrive at my destination having forgotten them. But as I biked away from those men, I realized this strategy was now failing me. My fists were clenched, knuckles white around the handlebars. My knees wobbled with each rotation. I was crying. I had absorbed their catcalls, and I felt a corrosive shame and anger building inside of me.

Being spoken down to and dehumanized is rote when you live in a visibly disabled body. There is no right way to respond. Most often a response feels impossible—sometimes because I cannot quickly volley back, or because I am alone and afraid of what would happen if I did engage. And when I am on my way to an eight-hour shift, it's too energetically costly. To ignore and forget it is all I can afford. Sometimes I have worried that this could be read as acquiescence or even agreement, that in my silence I am performing how ableism wants me to, silent and shrinking. I do not want to live in a world where disabled people continue to be institutionalized, mocked, harassed, and harmed. When I am unresponsive in the face of my own assault, am I permitting this world to flourish?

As a disabled person, I am able to stand and ambulate and communicate verbally. I am white and cisgender and middle class, and in these ways I am further privileged, my humanity more legible to the ableist viewer. How a group of young white men read me, as a thin, white, blonde woman is so different from how another disabled person would be read. And as I biked away, I wondered if I could use this legibility. I felt furious that my morning had been interrupted, and more furious still about the language that had been used against me. Disability looks many different ways, but there is a kinship that transcends these iterations. If these strangers could so assuredly dehumanize me, what would they say to my disabled kin?

I turned my wheel back toward the men, ready to unleash my anger. I wanted to slap them across the face with my words, make them feel fear with the strength of my vocabulary, my trusted tools as a nerd, in lieu of fists. But then I thought again, and turned back toward my destination. I did this three times, turning my wheel, then turning it back again. A part of me wanted to scream and kick and rip out some hearts and hair. The more rational part of me was aware that I am small and they were big, that I am a disabled woman and they were three able-bodied men. I was shaking with rage and fear, and they had seemed so self-assured. No matter the level of my anger, it would be unsafe to go back alone.

I eventually reached the diner, each rotation of the wheel having fuelled my fury, and by the time I joined my friends for breakfast, I was livid. My friends had already ordered. As I walked through the door, fried eggs and buttered toast were being delivered to the table. I slid into the booth as the plates were plunked down, and immediately streamed tears and snot from my face onto their morning meals. The breakfast grew cold as I spewed out all my feelings. My anger snowballed until we were all absorbed within it. We would not be soothed or placated. We would pool our rage and do something.

My friends were three women. As such, none of them were strangers to being yelled at on the street. While I am almost always yelled at for my training wheels, my friends are almost always yelled at for their bodies. When summer starts and soft skin is newly revealed to warm sunlight, each of us is freshly exposed. Like all feminine-presenting people, my friends cannot leave the house without getting shouted at from cars, cannot go out dancing without experiencing the familiar feeling of unfamiliar hands groping their waists. They change their outfits, rework their routes, and limit their movements. We have all been subjected to verbal harassment on account of ableism, sexism, and misogyny.

So, it was easy to get riled up together. All it took was the drop of one solitary tear and our collective experiences were on the table. We decided to harness those humiliations. This time, we would do it differently. We would not be silently subjected to hurtful words. We would call back. We left our eggs and some crumpled bills on the table, and headed back to the stoop where the men had been sitting.

We did not have a plan. None of us had ever been in a confrontation like this before. Most often when we are catcalled, we are alone, and the person shouting is in a car, speeding by. The chance to yell back is so rare, we were not sure how to use it. Would the men still be on the stoop? If they were, what would we say? Would we verbally threaten them? Would we stroll on by and catcall them?

We reached the stoop to find it empty. Normally, I would have left. The stoop, littered with beer cans and cigarette butts, was intimidating enough as it was. I could not imagine how I would feel if the men were still outside. I could not begin to imagine knocking on their door. But before I could turn away, my friend Layla was banging on the door, her fist ringing hard against it. One of the men came downstairs. He looked disgruntled and stoned.

"What do you want?" he asked us.

"I want to talk to you about the way that you verbally assaulted me earlier," I answered politely. Having not prepared, this was what came out. I sounded polite and a little meek. As my friends and I walked over, I had tried to pull up insults from the back of my memory. But insults barter in oppressive language or lean on threats of violence, neither of which suited me. Instead, I simply asked this man if we could speak.

The guy said he did not know what I was talking about. He said he had been outside all morning, and no one had "verbally assaulted" anyone. We argued, going back and forth, him calling me a liar and Layla responding that no one would make all of this up. Our voices got louder and louder as the debate continued, until eventually this man's friend, another guy from earlier, came downstairs and sided with his buddy. Eventually, the two men slammed the door on us, stating that we were "ruining their brunch."

We could have left. Instead, we got angrier.

"Fucking cowards!" we yelled. "Come down here and face us!" "Misogynist pigs!"

We screamed up to the second floor as we banged and kicked on the door. We were making a scene, and we didn't care. We were a loud and baleful chorus, one single, seething unit. As uncomfortable onlookers hurried by, we eventually won out. The two men came back downstairs.

"Look, it was us, okay?" one of the men conceded. "I yelled at you about your training wheels. I was stoned and I thought it was funny and I didn't think you would care. Now get over it, okay?" As he issued his begrudging apology, his friend stood silently by.

Get over it? It might sound absurd that someone could yell at a stranger and assume that they wouldn't mind, but I paused to consider his rationale. Has this been the presumption many others have made when I did not respond to their taunts? That I just didn't mind? That disabled people are so used to this behaviour, to constant othering, that we can tolerate it without discomfort? Or that as a femme I am so used to it, so used to having my body evaluated by men, that I can endure it without concern. I am sure that I have given this impression before, particularly given that as a disabled femme I am often acted upon as an object in social spaces.

As a response, "I do not mind" has kept me safe. I learned that if a doctor whose care I require makes an ableist comment about my body, it's best to grin and bear it if it means gaining access to the medical support I need.

How, now, to explain this to someone who had likely never been objectified in this way? So, I did as I've learned to do, and I began asking questions. Every time I come out from under anesthetic during a procedure, the first thing that I say to the attending nurse is, "Have you ever done this before?" Feeling physically undone, I need to know something about the others caring for me. Do you *know* this vulnerability? If they know the chill that accompanies waking up from surgery, I will trust them more because I can feel more certain of their empathy.

I hoped that by asking these men similar questions, we might build a connection, just long enough for them to understand what I had felt, if only because they had once felt something similar.

"Have you ever been yelled at by a stranger?"

"Have you ever been verbally assaulted?"

"Do you know what it's like to feel afraid and ashamed in public spaces?"

"Who has made you feel small before, and what did you do with their inflicted harm?"

"Did any part of you 'not mind?'"

I thought my invitations were eloquent, but the men just stared at me blankly.

"I told you I'm sorry. Now go home," the bigger man said. "I don't know what more you want from me."

He turned away from me and went inside the house. The other man looked at me sheepishly, shrugged and mumbled an apology, then went inside to join his buddy, closing the door in our faces.

I turned to my friends, unsure of whether to laugh or cry, whether to feel victorious or defeated. I had been so bowled over by adrenaline that I barely understood what had just happened, let alone how to respond to it.

We went back to the diner and continued our breakfast. We rehashed the incident, giddily lauding one another for our bravery.

If my hope had been to use my privilege to protect other disabled people, I couldn't be sure that I had been successful. Just as ignoring verbal violence can feel degrading, I had learned that so can trying to convince a bigot that you're deserving of care. I couldn't be sure this moment of incitement had been a win, but it had been something different. And perhaps difference is the best we can hope for, considering that there isn't a lot of room to win when you're being harassed by strangers.

Perhaps the best we can do is take care of ourselves and take care of our kin, and trust that a network of care is more powerful than the prejudiced slurs, that in loving protection we might render someone else's hatred meaningless.

That encounter did not lead to a seismic shift in how people see me and my beautiful red wheels. I still hear the taunts as I ride around town. I rarely respond, and worry less that my silence condones those harmful behaviours. If any of the offenders look closely enough, they'll see from my face that I refuse to be shamed. I sit in this refusal comfortably now because I understand myself as just one thread in a web of shameless disabled people and fierce femmes. By existing in our bodies in a world that wants to cause us harm, we are building a resistance, together.

What's In a Name? My Big, Wide Cunt

I spend a lot of time thinking about words. They are pretty important—we use them to say who we are, what we need, where we are going. "I am pregnant." "I don't love you." "We are out of toilet paper." These words strung together can really shake up your day.

When it comes to sex, there are lots of words to choose from. We can name our parts cookie, peepee, snatch, schlong, meat stick, or purple-headed monster. We may say we are horny, randy, or turned on. We can assert that we knocked boots, got intimate, or did the nasty. Considering that talking about sex is my job, I think about these kinds of words all the time. I weigh them, massage them with my tongue. The conclusion that these oral examinations have led me to is that a lot of sex-related words don't work for me. They don't match my desires, hug my curves, or fit between my legs. This has meant that over the last few years of selling sex toys and writing about sex, my vernacular has inevitably had to shift to better suit my needs. I have reappropriated and refurbished all sorts of words. I have put them in different places and ascribed to them different meanings to make them feel right. By now, I've got my own personal dictionary.

VAGINA vs. CUNT

Vagina, vagina, vagina. You may think it is an innocuous noun, safely medicalized and not too risqué. But many people don't even know what it means. I myself had been misled about the exact identity of the vagina for years.

As a teen, I felt an ambivalent about my vagina. As a part of my body, it appeared to be functioning normally. As a body part that has been tied to gender, I was aligned with my assignment and felt comfortable enough. I felt trepidation and fear about the ways in which men and boys seemed obsessed with vaginas, and this led to a kind of shutting down. So, as a teenager with a vagina I felt a kind of tempered curiosity. Then, in my early years of university, someone lent me Inga Muscio's *Cunt*, and my understanding of my vagina was completely rearranged. Reading her work was an initiation into feminism and gifted me one of those aha moments where I began to understand the underpinnings of patriarchy. And while those underpinnings are expansive, Muscio's book taught me something importantly specific: the vagina is just the hole.

The word "vagina" simply refers to that hole between your thighs. The fatty lips surrounding the hole—not part of the vagina. The nub near the top—it has a name of its own. All the sections that make up that part of the body are not just a vagina monolith but are instead a slew of individual parts. There are outer and inner labia that both offer protection. There is a cervix, a doughnut-looking thing that hands out at the back of the vaginal canal. There is a clitoris that seemingly has no function at all other than to feel really good. And below and in between all those parts is the vagina, just that little hole. It's an important hole—one that can push out blood and babies—but all the same, it remains just one small part of a much bigger thing.

This misnomer could be read as innocuous, an inconsequential simplification. But it could also be understood as an analogy for all the ways in which bodies designated "female" are reduced. A focus on the vagina turns the body into a hole to be penetrated. Attention is turned toward managing reproduction and away from the varied ways to find pleasure here.

At eighteen, learning about the misuse of the term vagina led me to the word vulva. Vulva. It means the genitals in their entirety, the whole damn thing. It felt like a perfect word. Reminiscent of a reliable European car, perhaps, but still rolled off the tongue. I loved it.

Youthful learning is righteous. I became a vulva zealot. I resolved to use the word vulva as often as possible, hoping it would incite revolutionary language shifts.

This lasted roughly three months. It took me about that long to realize that my change in vernacular wasn't changing the world order. This became especially apparent the day that I chose to tell my conservative bike mechanic that my bike seat was really hurting my vulva. I stood in front of him with my hands on my hips, wearing the shortest of short-shorts, and made my declaration.

"This bike seat is really making my vulva ache, man."

"Your what?!" he asked.

"My vulva," I repeated.

"I don't know what that is."

"You know, my vagina," I elaborated with a gesture south, even though my vagina was really not part of the problem.

"You mean your front pelvic bone," was his definitive and curt response, issued with a red face and awkward fumbles.

Evidently, a fifty-year-old man does not want to talk to me about my vagina nor learn the anatomically correct name for those parts. So, I decided to drop it. I would call it my vulva should the opportunity arise, but there was no need to bang it over everybody's heads.

Since then, I've stopped using the word vulva. It may be inclusive of all of my anatomical parts, but it just doesn't work for me anymore. The truth is, it isn't sexy. There is nothing even remotely hot about it. I do not want to tell my lover to touch my vulva, or worse, put her mouth on my vulva. "Baby, put your mouth on my vulva," sounds ridiculous, like I am asking her to taste a jello dish, the kind that has the chunks of stale cake and fruit floating in it. Instead, I've begun using the word cunt. My Big, Wide Cunt is actually what I call it (BWC for short).

Referring to our cunts as big and wide is a coping mechanism my co-worker Holly and I developed. We love talking about them, competing over the feats they can accomplish (no matter how exaggerated our claims).

"Dude, last night I had sex with the Vixen Outlaw."

"Whatever, girl, last night my girlfriend fisted me six times and I barely even felt it."

"Yeah, I've done that before. I've also pushed two babies out of my big, fat cunt, so you got nothing."

She always wins the competition. Babies trump everything. But we repeat the same old boasts to each other anyway. I would argue that we *have* to perform this ritualistic pissing contest if only to make sure we're still holding up okay. We have to celebrate the capacities of our cunts, revel in their expansive caverns and love them for their size. We have to argue over whose is bigger and tell each other facetious tales about the things they can hold. If we didn't do this, we may very well be convinced that the opposite is true: that size is bad, that we should want our vaginas to be small and tight.

There is so much messaging in the world telling us that there is only one desirable way to be, and we are exposed to this messaging in such a visceral way through our work at the sex shop. You can't talk to people about the most intimate parts of their bodies without being privy to a whole lot of body-shaming attitudes. And we talk to *so many* cisgender women who are ashamed of their vulvas. They are ashamed of how it looks. They worry that their clit is too big or too small, their labia too droopy or too lopsided, or their pubic hair too dark or too plentiful. They are ashamed of how it smells. Or they are ashamed of what it does and does not do: it does not come fast enough, it excretes too much, it doesn't ejaculate enough. And almost always people are worried that their vaginas are too loose. Being too loose is an ultimate vagina faux-pas in the pornified world we live in.

This shame is not any individual's fault. It makes total sense that women would hate their bodies in a world where we are taught to hate our bodies. Vulvas are to be shaved, douched, and tightened, not loved nor left ungroomed. To counter this vehement vulva-policing culture takes a lot of work and repetition. Holly and I remind ourselves daily that this constructed ideal of femininity is bunk, a mythology that we'd like to keep out of the folds of our underwear. We'll keep our cunts as big, wide, and hairy as we please.

FUCKING

Using the word cunt and adding the adjectives "big" and "wide" to the front of it was only the first step in the compilation of my own personal dictionary. The next entry was "fucking." I love the word fucking. Fah-king. The soft start and the harsh, guttural ending make it a perfect word, both as an adjective and a verb. As the former it can be wrathful: "You fucking asshole." Or commonplace: "So I'm talkin' to fackin' buddy over here..." As the latter it can be romantic: "We were fucking, and suddenly she paused and told me she loved me." Or insignificant: "Oh yeah, I fucked that guy. It was great." See, it's perfect, able to adapt to all moods and fit all situations. It is the meaning of the verb "to fuck" that I have had to reconsider.

I began thinking about what "fucking" really refers to shortly after starting work at the sex shop. You can't spend your days encountering so many variant human desires and ways of experiencing erotic pleasure and not re-examine your own preconceived notions of what "sex" is. So, in my confusion, I turned to Google.

Let me quote the Wikipedia definition for sexual intercourse: "Sexual intercourse (or coitus or copulation) is a sexual activity typically involving the insertion and thrusting of the penis into the vagina for sexual pleasure or reproduction. This is also known as vaginal intercourse or vaginal sex. Other forms of penetrative sexual intercourse include anal sex (penetration of the anus by the penis), oral sex (penetration of the mouth by the penis or oral penetration of the female genitalia), fingering (sexual penetration by the fingers), and penetration by use of a dildo (especially a strap-on dildo)."

Huh. While I sort of appreciate the shout out to queer folks, this definition still leaves me with so many questions. For instance: What if a penis enters my vagina but I don't experience sexual pleasure? What if the penis was only in my vagina for, like, a second? Is there a time limit on this kind of thing? Or what if someone gets off solely through external stimulation and there is no penetration involved? Is it still intercourse if nothing is put in any hole whatsoever? And what if there are four people involved rather than a pairing? Or only one person involved? Is this all a numbers game? Our societal definitions of "fucking" are so limiting. Why does it always have to be about a pair and about penetration? Why does it have to be about genitals at all? By having such a narrow definition, we are only putting restrictions on our ideas about pleasure. We are regulating who has the right to feel good and how.

And so, I have redefined the word "fucking" for myself. I have made it bigger and broader and better. When I write, think, and talk about fucking, I am not referring exclusively to penises and vaginas, or penetration, or even orgasms. Fucking, I believe, is an act, and I mean any act, which can be performed alone or consensually with one or more partners, with the ultimate aim of giving and receiving erotic pleasure.

Fucking can mean being stretched out naked on the bed with someone else's hand in your big, wide cunt.

Fucking can mean rubbing your nose against someone else's thigh.

Fucking can mean giving blow jobs.

Fucking can mean masturbating.

Fucking can mean making out.

Fucking can mean breathing deep and thinking the dirtiest of dirty thoughts, if that's how you get off.

The point is that fucking should be about *feeling erotic pleasure*. It should not be about the pressure to orgasm, to make someone else orgasm, to have a partner, or to look hot. If fucking is defined as feeling erotic pleasure, then it can better include all kinds of people, with all kinds of sexualities, bodies, and abilities. I know this is broad, but what's wrong with broad? Why can't we flip our definitions and expand our ideas?

And though I find this kind of rewriting exciting, I recently received the following email from my grandmother:

Hi my dear granddaughter,

I'm sure that I already wrote to comment on your great ability with words. I just saw your blog post. You write really well. You are going to do a superlative job of your book, whatever the topic. My only quibble would be with some language, principally the "F" word because of its shock value. When used in a wonderful part of life that you wish to normalize and make accessible for all, its use may turn away individuals who you are actually anxious to reach. Just a thought from your old Grandmother, who is admittedly many generations removed from the mainstream in 2013.
—Grandma, 2013

Let me describe to you my grandmother. She is a genius of an eighty-three-year-old woman who can navigate the world of Facebook, blogs, and the internet at large. Like grandmothers in fairy tales, she is soft and good for hugging, has filled me with baked goods my entire life, and is endlessly kind. She has never had a drink. She does not smoke nor gamble, nor has she ever had her ears pierced. Having been an elementary school teacher her entire life, she is well-versed in offering supportive and gentle criticisms. And imagining her reading my blog makes me cringe with embarrassment.

I considered my grandma's suggestion and realized that she makes a valid point. These words I use do not work for her, or for most people of her generation, many of whom I am sure are having sex and could probably use some sex education. To be fair, if I were speaking with an eighty-three-year-old woman about sex, I would probably not say the word "fucking" to her, nor describe myself as having a big, wide cunt. When writing about sex on the internet, I often imagine my audience as being significantly younger and perhaps more acquainted with my particular style of speech. But my grandmother kindly reminded me that all words have their place, even those that do not match my wants.

When I am sitting at the tiny round table in my kitchen, being vulgar fits best. It makes me feel powerful and tough-as-fuck to control my language. But when I am working in a sex shop and customers come in nervous and uncertain, there is no need to impress them with my filthy vernacular. Just as discussing my needs with my bike mechanic is not necessarily a teachable moment regarding anatomical correctness. In those instances, softer words make the most sense. I will even use the words pee-pee, cookie, and front pelvic bone if that is really what someone needs to hear to feel comfortable. My words can bend to suit any stranger. We all shift our shapes and presentations for different audiences as we navigate our own personal universe. Words, in all their power, are malleable and made to be redefined.

Looking For Blood

Everything was going so well that, of course, something bad would happen. I was embracing my sexuality, learning about desire, and feeling safe and secure in my body. It seemed as though I had sussed out and then annihilated any and all internalized shame that I had acquired surrounding sex. I had learned that sex could be so much more than just awkward, and that there was no "right" way to do it. I had learned exactly how to make myself feel good and how to exert my sexual agency. I was feeling in control of my body, on top of the world, and entirely self-certain. And then it happened.

A letter from a friend written to me during that time sums it up best: "Sometimes, you just trip and get pregnant." That is exactly how it felt. Not to remove all of my agency—I did actively make choices and consciously had a lapse in my good judgement. As we are all guilty of doing, I momentarily mistook myself as immortal (or, more topically, infertile) and threw myself full throttle into risks and danger and thoughtless moments of sex. I gave every inch of myself to those fucks, let my skin feel it all, held him inside of me and felt completely in control while choosing to relinquish all control. But still, when I took that test, when the first stick and then the second, third, and fourth each turned up their mean little plus signs, it felt just like I had tripped. That pothole came out of nowhere and sent me staggering.

And so, I was pregnant. And I was going to have an abortion. I was probably the one billionth person in the world to have been in this position. I was certainly not the first. What I experienced was not new or unique in any way. And by all means, my trials and tribulations were undoubtedly far easier than those of the people who came before me. Thanks to so many radical fighters, I did not have to use a coat hanger nor be ushered into a back alleyway. Instead, I was able to legally have an abortion in a safe hospital at no financial cost. In the grand scheme of things, I was lucky. But I definitely did not feel lucky.

To say that I "staggered" is perhaps being retrospectively optimistic. It would really be more accurate to write that pregnancy was akin to being violently knocked flat on my face and losing all of my teeth. My pregnancy days were one long, cruel, meandering nightmare. It was an incredibly difficult experience, not because I did not want to have an abortion, but because it felt as though the rest of the world did not want me to. I was experiencing firsthand the ways in which patriarchal state-sanctioned structures limit the ability of people with vulvas to make choices which directly affect our bodily autonomy. It's a fucked-up thing to move through and to be so viscerally affected by. You can't live through it and not be changed.

I found out for sure on September 3. Which was three days after August 30. Which was my twenty-fifth birthday. So maybe I should begin there. August 30 was my twenty-fifth birthday, and on that day my period was four days late. It was four days late, which was unusual, and I was concerned. But it was my birthday, the sun was shining, and I was committed to not worrying about it just yet. I woke up early that day and went straight to the lake. It was seven a.m. and the sun was already hot on my back. I remember that I had the rocky shore all to myself, an unexpected solitude that I mistook as a good omen. Feeling hopeful about the coming year, I plunged my body into the cool water and did my own informal baptism ceremony. I rebirthed myself and came out of Long Lake one year older. As I lay drying in the sun, my phone rang. It was my mom. My grandfather had died, and I had to come home. I was on a plane within hours.

For three days, I was in Ontario at the old farmhouse. It was so hot. We were all sticky and uncomfortable, our bellies full of community casseroles and our hearts full of grief. The whole family was there, milling around. No one knew what to say or where to sit. In between meals and amidst small talk, my grandfather was buried. After the ceremony, we all swapped our suits for overalls, headed out to the barn, and stayed there all night soothing tears with whisky. We laughed and cried. We retold the same familiar anecdotes to comfort one another. I don't remember much of the stories we told, to be honest. I was always missing the punchline anyway. I was too busy sneaking off, ducking into bathrooms and empty bedrooms. There I would pull down my pants to examine my underwear, put my fingers inside myself, looking for blood. Each time there was nothing.

On September 3, two days after burying my grandfather and three days after turning twenty-five, my period was seven days late. I got on a plane and flew back to Nova Scotia. I arrived in the city by late afternoon and went straight to the pharmacy. I picked up a pregnancy test, and it felt weirdly as though my life had become a moment stolen from an early episode of *Degrassi High*. It felt silly and surreal, imagining that I was probably taking myself too seriously. But still, I was too nervous to open the box.

I brought the test home and put it on a shelf. On the day my grandfather died I had been in the middle of moving into a new apartment. So now I had returned to an unfamiliar home feeling disjointed, unsure of where things went.

I ignored the test for hours and busied myself unpacking boxes. I felt alone. The place was small and old. There was not enough light. My stuff did not seem to fit into the corners. I unloaded boxes, positioned my things, and repositioned them again. Still, nothing fit. Still, the pregnancy test sat there waiting.

I spent the whole night unpacking boxes and shuffling and reshuffling furniture. By midnight there was really only one thing left to do. With every item in its place, there were no more distractions or excuses. I took the test.

This is what happens when you take a pregnancy test. First, you harness your courage. Second, you step into vulnerability and pull down your pants. Third, you hover above the toilet in a position that will allow you to pee on a stick. You want to hit the stick in the right spot, but you also don't want to accidentally piss on your hand, or have bounce back and get piss all over the seat. This process seemed awkward to me, especially considering that when I pee I am already using one hand for my catheter. I decided to simplify the process and pee into a jar. I squatted down and let loose right over a mason jar which had, according to the label, contained dill pickles in 2007. Remarkably, this really did feel less awkward. Then I dipped the stick in and waited. Fourth, you must wait for two full minutes. I chose to leave the stick in the bathroom alone, with the door shut. Despite being an inanimate object, I wanted to give the stick some privacy while it determined my fate.

Over the next ten minutes, I dipped four sticks into that

jar. The sticks, independently of one another, each arrived at the same conclusion: I was pregnant. Pregnancy tests do not give false positives. If they say yes, they mean it. And so, I defied the arid vastness of my corneas. Despite the funeral and all that had happened, I still had some salt water reserves. I cried all night.

Realizing I was pregnant was heartbreaking and scary, but it was not a conundrum. It was so easy to make my decision that it almost felt as though I didn't even make one. As soon as I had an inkling that I was pregnant, I knew that if the worst were true I would have an abortion. I had always been pro-choice, long before I had even identified as a feminist. For as far back as I could remember, it had just seemed intuitive to me that a person should be able to choose what to do with their body. No argument that operated under the thesis that someone should not be able to exert control over their own fertility had ever made much sense to me. I had always thought the opposition to abortions was a completely absurd throwback from the not-so-distant past where the complete subjugation of women went unquestioned. Denying someone access to abortion seemed comparable to denying women the right to vote: a totally wacky expression of patriarchy that insinuated that people with vulvas cannot be trusted with anything. I did not have to work through any moral dilemma. I felt sad, scared, and alone, but I was certain. I called the doctor's office the very next day to book my appointment.

When you are expecting an abortion in Nova Scotia, there are multiple hoops you must jump through. First, you must get an abortion referral. Then, you must get blood work and an ultrasound done. Then, you must wait an extended period of time. Finally, you are permitted to have the procedure. I went into my first hoop, the appointment for a referral, entirely unprepared. Which is to say that I went in prepared to get what I wanted, only to find out that while I had the right to choose, I did not get to choose all that much.

I went to the health centre that day well dressed and feeling armoured. As a disabled person, I had already been a patient for sixteen years. This meant that I was well versed in navigating the twisted bureaucracy of the medical health system. I knew how to advocate for myself in an environment that has consistently labelled me as less than. I knew to approach the medical industrial complex from a position of distrust, had learned to walk into a room primed for conflict. And I had figured out how to get my needs met. I dress up. I speak eloquently. I lean on my access to privilege: I use being a white, educated, middle-class cisgender woman to my advantage. I went to my first appointment expecting to do just that. I knew exactly what I wanted, and I wanted it badly. I imagined that I would go in, explain the situation, and be scheduled for an abortion a week later. Unfortunately, that is not what happened. Having an abortion was not nearly that simple.

I entered the clinic to find the waiting room empty. I registered at the front desk and sat down on the plasticized chairs trying to look proper. I flipped through magazines, picked my nails, and tapped my toes on the stained carpet. I had been so sure that this appointment would be fast and efficient that I had scheduled myself to go into work immediately afterwards. At this point in my pregnancy, I was under the impression that if I just kept really busy, working all the time, then I would be able to ignore my glaringly absent period and pretend that nothing was amiss. So, I willed the doctor to hurry. I did not want to have to be still for any amount of time; I avoided all possible moments of reflection.

Eventually the nurse called me in, and thus began my hoop jumping. The first step is to go into a room to discuss your situation. A nurse asks you questions about who you are and how you feel. They ask about your menstrual cycle, your sexual partners, and how far along you think you may be. Then the nurse explains each of your options: to have a baby, to give a baby up for adoption, or to have what is called a therapeutic abortion, or TA. As I stumbled through our conversation and took in all of this information, I wondered if this was standard protocol for all pregnant people. If someone were to call the doctor and say they were pregnant and wanted to keep the baby, would they still need to discuss their options? Would the doctor suggest having an abortion? Or is it only if you are on the other side of the coin that you need to really consider these things? Either way, I knew exactly what I was doing. I had already told the nurse why I was here. But these steps were required, so I sat through them obediently, expecting this conversation would lead directly to my appointment.

When the nurse finished her explanations and I reaffirmed that I would definitely be having an abortion, I was given an information packet and ushered into a second room. This room had an examination table, and I was told to remove my pants and underwear and put my feet in the cold, metal stirrups. I hoped that this would be it, something would happen on that table, and I would walk out of the clinic free of all problems. Instead, the doctor came in and put her gloves on. She explained that she was going to check and see how far along I was, and then she put her latex-clad fingers inside my vagina and pressed up against my cervix.

"Three weeks," she said as she pulled out and snapped her gloves off. I was floored. While I had assumed that I was about that far along, hearing it from someone else's mouth allowed the reality to sink in that much deeper. It startled me that someone could touch my body and know that much. I wondered if others would be able to tell. Was it so obvious? Would I show? The sense of self-assuredness I had walked in with was waning, and I was too baffled to ask these questions aloud. The doctor told me to put my clothes back on and return to the first room. I was a yo-yo, going back and forth. I zipped up my jeans and zipped back to the first room. There, the same nurse as before reminded me again of my options. I again chose abortion. The nurse then explained to me what exactly would happen next: I would be referred to have an ultrasound and blood test at the hospital—to make sure that the pregnancy was not showing any complications—and then I would have "the procedure." She explained that the procedure would take place in a private wing of the hospital. I nodded my understanding as all of this was explained. And then the nurse told me, "Okay, so we will have you booked in for October 5."

"What do you mean?" I asked. I could not imagine why I would need to come back and visit the clinic in a month's time.

"That is when you will have your TA. On October 5, at the hospital."

"That isn't for another month!"

"That's standard. We prefer the patient be pregnant for at least seven weeks to ensure the procedure takes. By October 5, you should be about seven and a half. Additionally, there is a long wait time considering we're serving Prince Edward

Island and often New Brunswickers. Seven weeks is the earliest we could possibly see you."

"That can't be right! No way! I work full time. I can't just hang out and be unwillingly pregnant for another four weeks."

I was panicking. I had already known I was pregnant for five days and found it to be awful. I had not experienced any symptoms yet, but just knowing that something was growing in my body, something that I did not want, was very disconcerting. My bodily autonomy was feeling wildly compromised, and I was yearning for that hungry little zygote to be out of me. I could not imagine just letting it gestate in there for another twenty-eight days.

But it was going to. No matter how upset I was or how much I argued, I did not have the power to change my wait time. The nurse kindly explained to me that there was really no way of adjusting the timing. It was just the way things were. She reassured me that pregnant people do things all the time and I would not have to put my life on pause. She said it would be unlikely that I would even experience any symptoms. "You'll be fine," she said.

I left the clinic feeling defeated and angry. I felt as though I was being punished on a State level. I knew that in other provinces there was not such a lengthy wait time. I had friends who had had abortions in Toronto, and they had been able to have the procedure within a week of finding out. And I knew other people who had gotten pregnant on the west coast and had had access to medical abortions, where they did not have to wait or be hospitalized, but had instead taken an oral pill. This East Coast experience was feeling comparatively draconian.

I believed the nurse when she said the wait time was largely an issue of logistics. Accessing any kind of medical service on the impoverished East Coast has never been easy. But it also felt like I had incurred a penalty, as though waiting was a forced period of reflection. It all felt so paternalistic. As an adult, I had the tools to understand that actions have consequences. I knew what I wanted. I knew about remorse. I also knew how to forgive myself. I did not need to be taught these lessons.

I went into my wait time kicking up against it. I felt so angry that I thought I would surely be angry for the full four weeks. But that didn't happen. Getting pregnant was a lesson in many things—in learning to adjust my expectations and to practise patience. The futility of raging at a system that you are powerless to rectify is disheartening. Not to mention that being pregnant zapped everything out of me. I was too tired to be anything other than tired. Instead of being righteous, I became exhausted and embarrassed. The silence around abortion stifled me, and I began to doubt myself. Not my decisions, but my own self. I had a sense that I had erred, that I was wrong for getting pregnant with a virtual stranger, that I should have known better. Shame around abortion is so pervasive and so seductive.

Your body may go through a lot of different things during the first nine weeks of pregnancy. I do not profess to know all of them, but I can tell you what I felt. I felt hunger. I could eat absolutely everything, except vegetables. If it was a carb and within five feet of me you could expect it to be in my mouth. With renewed vigor, I loved macaroni and cheese, pasta, and cereal. I could eat an entire loaf of sourdough for breakfast. Paired with this new hunger was a heightened sense of smell. While it is probably some evolutionary by-product intended to help sniff out life-threatening predators, I used it to suss out sweets. I followed my nose to every cake, cookie, and crumpet in the city and promptly shoved them into my pie-hole.

When I wasn't eating, I was fast asleep. It felt like I could sleep forever. Fourteen hours a night became my norm, and I would still wake up tired in the morning. I would drag my body to work and then back to my bed. So much for keeping busy and distracting myself—it seemed impossible to do anything other than what was absolutely necessary.

There were so many things that signalled that my body was no longer all my own. My breasts swelled and felt misshapen. My vulva smelled strong and musky. (I spent the duration of my pregnancy with my legs crossed, irrationally afraid that if I opened them, someone would smell my fertility). The smell of coffee and cigarettes, my two most favoured vices, became abhorrent. The mornings became a time when I would vomit. The nights became a time when I would cry. The afternoons could not be predicted. I was completely out of control.

I spent a lot of that time alone. We are taught not to speak about abortions, and I followed the rules. When people asked how I was doing, I would smile, and nod, and talk about the weather. I would lie. How could I be honest? Should I have answered that I was pregnant? It was strange and burdensome to be holding on to this secret. I have never held secrets. But I did not think I could talk about this one thing. So it stayed secret, and I stayed isolated. Secrets will do that. They turn you into a lonely island.

And then October 5 came, and suddenly it was all over, just like that.

The night before my abortion it rained and rained. I repainted my walls, replacing the white emptiness with

Egyptian Sunrise—a warm orange. It had felt like I ought to either paint my walls or shave my head, that I should do something outward to mark my massive internal shift. Vanity has forever barred head shaving as an option for me, so painting was all that was left. When I woke up on October 5, it was to the smell of paint drying on sticky walls.

It was 5:30 a.m., and the sky was still dark and sunless. Two friends and I crowded into my car. I lay down in the back seat. My abortion was unfortunately scheduled during the Forty Days for Life protests, forty days every year during which anti-choice activists stand outside of hospitals and clinics across North America, shaming those of us who have had to make the difficult choice to terminate a pregnancy. It is a truly detestable vigil they hold, mourning the deaths of "babies" without any consideration for the pain that those of us who are pregnant may be experiencing, and disregarding our right to choose what happens to our bodies. Predictably, the protests are populated primarily by old, cisgender white men. Men with bodies that have never been pregnant, with bodies that have never had their reproductive rights denied. I lay down in my back seat as we drove up to the City Hospital, not to protect myself from their judging eyes but to protect them from my forceful fists. Without a doubt, if I had looked at them right then, with all the pain I was holding and all the exhaustion I was feeling, I would have let loose. I would have missed my abortion appointment to lay all of my wrath on their old, bigoted bones. I could have left it there with them, my rage and my hurt and my fury, and walked away lighter. But instead, I ducked down in my back seat and saved my strength for myself. My abortion was more important.

Inside the hospital, I was separated from my friends and led through a strange fluorescent maze. The abortion division is laid out at the end of a windowless sequence of tunnels designed to hide and protect the staff. Performing abortions was dangerous, and sometimes still is, and so the doctors and the nurses and those of us who are pregnant were all hidden from the outside world. My friends were sent to one waiting room, and I was brought through the maze to another. I waited with other women for a couple of hours. One of us would be called up, led away, and would not come back. Again, I bit my nails. Again, I pretended to read the magazines. Eventually, it was my turn.

"Kaleigh Trace."

I stood up, solemn. I followed the nurse into another room and was given a locker. I took off all of my clothes and put on a long, green gown, then progressed into a third room, where I was offered drugs.

"Opiates, Ativan, or nothing at all?" the nurse asked.

Part of me wanted to choose nothing at all. This was going to be one of the biggest moments of my life, and I wanted to experience it sober, without a clouded mind or a subdued heart. But as I weighed my decision, I realized my fingertips were caked in blood because I had bitten my nails down to the quick. I noticed that my knees were shaking, and I was holding on to the wall for support. It was clear that I did not quite have my shit together. So, I obediently took the small paper cup of Ativan and swallowed.

Shortly thereafter I was led into the fourth and final room. Again, just like during my very first appointment, I was presented with cold metal stirrups to place my feet in. I lay down on the bed cloaked in crinkly paper and got into position. Above me, three fluorescent bulbs beamed down and hurt my eyes. I began to cry, afraid that I would just lie in that room alone while a machine performed some painful procedure. I had no idea what to expect, but the white walls and the smell of disinfectant were not reassuring. Luckily, that is not how abortions are performed. It is not a wordless operation acted out by inanimate, cold, beeping machinery. For something so painful, it was an event that felt deeply human and tender.

A nurse came in and held my hand and spoke to me through it all. She encouraged me to look into her eyes and not down at the doctor between my legs. She issued me reassurances about my choice, about my strength, about being a good woman. Throughout all of it she never let go of my hands, even when the vacuuming began and I squeezed so hard that I thought I heard her fingers crack. She squeezed back, and stroked my hair, and kept murmuring to me as the doctor moved in and out of the room, brusquely explaining what was happening. In total, the procedure itself must have taken less than ten minutes. Just like that, my womb was emptied and my body was all mine again.

That same nurse put me in a chair and wheeled me into the recovery room, where I was given milk and cookies and a snack pack of cheese and crackers. The food, in its neat packaging and tiny portions, felt like snacks meant for primary school kids on lunch break. Throughout all of this, I could not stop sobbing. I slobbered into the cheese and crackers. I swallowed the snacks like they were medicine, tasting nothing but my own mucus. The nurse stayed with me as I ate, and cried, and bled onto my gown. It was not a glamorous moment. It did not matter. No one asked me why I was crying or told me to stop. It was a place accustomed to tears, and so I gave in to them fully.

Half an hour later, I was with my friends again, ready to go back out into the world. I ducked down in my back seat, and we went out the way we had come in, as though nothing had changed, though everything had.

It all happened just like that. One morning it was over. Yet, while my body had been returned to me, my emotional self was still searching for ground. I had remained so quiet during my pregnancy. I had feared people's reactions and the impact that any judgment might have had on me during a time of great vulnerability. My disabled body had always been spoken about in social spaces, and I had learned how to control the narrative. But by not speaking about my abortion, I lost this source of power, and shame had taken root. I started to speak. To friends, family, at rallies and counter-protests. I told my own story, and, in that ownership, I found healing.

I refuse to believe that I was wrong for having an abortion. Instead, I think I was brave, and I am proud of myself and all of us who have moved through that experience. We are strong, and we are many. Abortions are not rare. It is remarkable and tragic that something so commonplace is still so inaccessible and legislated against, that it still needs to be spoken about in hushed voices.

The more I talk about my experience, the more it transforms from MY ABORTION into my abortion, something I lived through but that does not define me. Each word that leaves my mouth takes with it some weight off my shoulders. Speaking my abortion out loud is an offering to the self who felt she needed to keep a secret. I want to use words to deconstruct old ideas. I want to use words to lay new foundations for new attitudes, ones that are more kind. I want to learn from my experience and share it so we can all learn. I want others who may have an abortion to be able to walk into it with their heads up and their hearts strong and their mouths wide open, shouting their own words and stories out into the world. Together, our shared stories can coalesce and become a force so strong that no one can stop us.

Queer Fits Right Between My Legs

I am a queer, disabled woman. I say it with complete certainty. But this has taken a long, long time. I've been peeling those labels on and off my chest for nineteen years. I've rearranged them (queer woman with a disability), altered them (bi-curious dis/abled woman), and added to them (queer, disabled, sex-positive, femme, cisgender woman). Ultimately, queer, disabled woman feels best (for right now).

I was in my car accident in 1995. This is when I sustained my spinal cord injury that effectively led me to being a person with a disability. Since that time, I have had my swaying legs, my indomitable bladder, and my chronic pain. Since that time, the world has looked at me as I've teetered through my life and called me disabled—I definitely do not live up to an able-bodied norm. I am not normal.

I initially did not even *like* this truth, let alone love it as I do now. As a kid, I completely rejected that label. I could see no reason for wanting to embrace a word that seemed synonymous with weaker, lesser than, and unattractive. Like most kids, all I wanted was to fit in. So, I learned quickly how to hide and disregard my differences. I wore clothing and shoes that I hoped would draw attention away from my leg braces. At recess and in gym class I would "run" around with the other kids, stumbling after them with my quad canes as support. I would make an effort at soccer, tree-climbing, and dodge ball. I would laugh off all my trips and falls. I would do absolutely anything to be just like everyone else.

This drive only grew as I entered the homogenizing social force that is high school. As soon as I set foot in the ninth grade, I knew that there was no way I wanted to be noticed as "different." I wanted popularity, boyfriends, and all of those good times I had seen in *Dazed and Confused*, *Empire Records*, and *She's All That*.

The first shaky step toward this end was to stop using my cane. Up until this point, my mother had been painstakingly painting my canes to match my outfits: one was baby-doll pink with glitter, and another was blue with little white clouds spread out across it. This no longer mattered to me. I knew that having a walking aid would draw the wrong kind of attention and annihilate any chance at getting a date. The year prior, my first ever boyfriend had dumped me when his older brother had teased him about dating the "gimpy girl." It was crucial that this not happen again. So, I would use my cane to get on the bus and then hide it in my locker all day. When I was strong enough, I stopped using it altogether. I would risk any tumble to not have it. I was certain that without it, I was passing.

During high school, I wobbled through every field party, barn party, and tailgate party. No matter how rocky and uneven the terrain, I would go where everyone else was going and do what everyone else was doing. I would get shit-faced; hit the bong; jump into dark, rocky quarries; and do whatever it took to fit in. For the most part, I was happy. It felt like I was living the life I had seen in the movies. I had boyfriends and nice clothes, and I went to parties. My disability did not go unnoticed, but I was able to access enough spaces to make it so that it seemed not to affect me. I could do almost everything the other kids did. I never once called myself disabled. I was just like everyone else. And no matter how much my feet hurt or my back ached at the end of the night, I always thought it was worth it.

Then I left small-town Ontario. Moving to a city across the country necessitated change. I no longer had my old station wagon to get me around or my brother to carry my books. The university I was attending was an indecipherable maze of long hallways and spiral staircases. I was living in a residence full of other drunk eighteen-year-olds who would trek for kilometres to the bar downtown. I was trying to ride city buses that did not allow you to stop for a pee break. Everything was suddenly a million times more difficult. The conceptual fallacy that I had been embracing for years was facing its reckoning: I was not like everybody else.

Within six months of leaving home, I began calling myself "a person with a disability." The facts were too clear to ignore: I could not make it to class on time, could not walk as fast as my friends, and did not want to ride the city bus for fear of peeing my pants. So, like any stranger in a new place, I was given the option to reinvent myself, and I chose to move in a more honest direction. I slowly turned to disability, and I looked at it, head on.

I started reading disability theory and seeking representations of myself. As I learned about the disability movement, I began to understand the ways that I had internalized an ableist culture. As I read critical disability theorists such as Catherine Frazee and Mia Mingus, I slowly but surely undid some of the knots I had tied around my heart. I slowly but surely looked at my crooked feet and fell in love with them. I slowly but surely grew more comfortable asking for help. I began to love myself in my entirety. I began to reclaim what it meant for me to have a spinal cord injury. I began to love calling myself disabled. I no longer wanted to reproduce ableist oppression by denying my identity. I no longer wanted to try to be something I was not.

Within the disabled community, I embody a lot of privilege. I can access most inaccessible spaces. I can stand upright, communicate verbally, and use my whiteness and neurotypicality to my advantage. This privilege must be noted. Disability is so broad, and ableism can affect us in so many different ways. The way that I experience disability has meant that I lived without fully recognizing it for a long time. And so the route I took to arrive at lovingly calling myself disabled was a long and winding one. I had to recognize the fucked-up shit I had ignorantly done, and I had to rework so many of my own damaging beliefs. I am still working on all of this. In many ways I have not yet "arrived" anywhere. While I proudly call myself a disabled woman, there is still so much I am learning, and there are so many ways in which I am still growing.

Coming to call myself queer has been a similarly serpentine path. It was not straightforward nor immediate. I flirted with the term *queer* for years. For most of my life I had been eyeing its broad shoulders and wondering if I would fit into its plaid shirts.

I grew up surrounded by lesbians. I'm not exaggerating. They were literally everywhere. They lived in my basement and attended all my family parties. Gay women essentially were my family parties. I come from one big, noisy, pretty gay matriarchy. My mother has fourteen siblings, and those fourteen siblings collectively birthed forty-one blonde-haired, blue-eyed, round-bottomed babies. Most of those babies were girls (twenty-six, to be exact) and all of those girls learned quickly how to be loud.

My mother and her sisters have always ruled the roost. If you were to ask a Lalonde "who's the boss?" my mother and each of her sisters would answer that they are. They are women in control, and they taught their daughters that skill—or maybe we all just contracted it by osmosis. Lalonde girls are always in charge, they tell the most vulgar jokes, and they have a penchant for being queerer than a two-dollar bill. A whole slew of my cousins are bona fide, brilliant gay women.

Within this matriarchal structure, I was the thirty-sixth little bundle of fatty, pink flesh rolls to be popped out. This means that I have always been one of the youngest of the pack. I have spent the duration of my life thus far following around my older, smarter, cooler cousins. I wore Converse sneakers because they wore Converse sneakers. I played tee-ball because they played tee-ball. I listened to Prince because they listened to Prince. My identity has essentially always just been one epic act of mimicry. So being queer has always been an option, if not even an inevitability, for me. As a kid I had never thought of it as a particularly strange, scary, or dangerous identity to embrace. And still it took me years to arrive here, at calling myself by its name.

Perhaps predictably, my desires started to veer off the straight and narrow path shortly after beginning work at Venus Envy. I don't think it was Venus Envy exactly that made me gay, but rather being surrounded by an almost entirely queer staff every day helped suss out and fertilize those deeply rooted queer feelings. Within six months of working there, my fantasies were getting all jumbled up and confused. I started looking at everyone a little differently. I would cock my head at every queer-looking person who walked into the shop and wonder if I was attracted to them or if I just wanted to be them. At first, I thought I was maybe just homesick for my big, lesbian family and was feeling drawn to dykes on account of that. I could not quite figure it out.

And then came my first Big Gay Crush. I became obsessed with a woman named Jane. We met at a potluck of a friend of a friend. She was just passing through town and had nowhere to stay. By the end of our five-minute, introductory conversation, I selflessly offered to share my bed with her. She slurped a noodle from her bowl of vegan pad thai, shrugged her shoulders, and said, "Sure."

She stayed with me for weeks. I would lie beside her at night, literally shaking. Her back to me, I would look at the curve of her spine and will myself not to touch her. Even being near her would sometimes make me want to puke. My attraction was so painfully visceral that for a short time I was truly convinced not that I was gay, but that I had the stomach flu. It was raw and all-consuming. It was also a totally unsustainable emotional state to live in. I had to tell her. So, one night I got drunk at the gay bar and confessed my baby-gay, butterfly feelings.

"Listen, we need to talk about what's going on here. I think we should kiss," I declared both boldly and sloppily, as my drink sloshed around in my cup.

Jane looked at me with pity, explained that straight girls weren't her type, and left town a few days later.

That was it. She was gone as fast as she had come, and I was one crushed puppy. With Jane's blunt rejection and departure, my gay feelings faded. I assumed that she was probably right. For an embarrassingly long time, I believed that queer people could somehow sense their own kind, as if everyone was equipped with a gay divining rod. I trusted Jane's judgment of me. I must be straight. All the signs pointed that way. For instance, I wore dresses. In my childhood I had been obsessed with Barbies, ponies, and princesses. I loved lipstick and nail polish. I listened to folky indie pop. In no way did I match up to the image of queer that I had come to understand through watching my cousins and my co-workers.

I have learned everything from books. So, post-Jane and reeling from my crush, I turned to queer theory. I read *Brazen Femme*, *Whipping Girl*, and *Persistence*. I looked for versions of me in these books. I wanted to learn about expressions of queerness that looked different from those I had always known. I wanted to hear from the experts. Could I be queer? Did it still count if I had such long hair? As I read more diverse portrayals of queerness and femininity, I began to question exactly why I was so reluctant to call myself queer.

For a long time I had assumed that the way that I looked, coupled with my attraction to masculinity, implied an obvious straightness. Plus, I knew so many powerful people who had struggled and fought for the label queer that I did not want to appropriate it; I did not want to take on an identity that was not rightfully mine. I had internalized femmephobic notions of what it means to be gay, notions that limited queer women to looking and acting a particular way. I had so strongly come to believe that queer could only mean a few things that I had been overlooking the importance of queering femininity. I had not understood that I could wear my curls long and my skirts short with a brazen toughness that had nothing to do with heteronormativity. Queer could look my way too.

Much like with *disabled*, I came to *queer* through an undoing. I undressed the grey pantsuit of my femmephobia and instead put on a sparkly, hot-pink mini skirt. Now, I know that queer fits. Queer makes space for my crisscrossing legs, my flaming-red lipstick, and my big hair. In queerness I can have a kind of sex that denies any kind of trajectory or framework, a kind of sex that allows for the complexities of disability and gender. Queer leans left with my politics and fits right between my legs. I am a disabled, queer femme, and I love queer bodies.

The labels *queer* and *disabled* fit well together, and I am honoured to hold them both. They fit together because they both involve resistance. Resistance against those tired ideas of what and how one should be, resistance against presumed and ill-fitting "truths" about the world. In this resistance, both of these words work to create a much-needed space: space for bodies to be valued in and of themselves, space for beauty and love to be redefined.

A Work of Erotica: Fuck Me Anywhere

It all began with a bout of unsatisfactory sex. Nobody was knocking on my door, and my own hands weren't getting the job done. I had just experienced my first queer heartbreak, and I was convinced that I would never have sex with another person again. Instead, I was spending most of my time feeling sad and eating ice cream. After crying at work, again, I decided that something had to be done. I turned to erotica. Watching porn has never really done it for me, even radical queer porn. My attention span is too short. But I hoped that reading erotica might be different. I borrowed some books from the shop, grabbed a fresh bottle of lube, and went home to try my luck.

My hopes were misplaced. Reading erotic literature had the opposite of its intended effect on my libido. If there had been any juices to begin with, they would have surely dried up. Essentially, the erotica was abhorrent. Bad. Really bad. In cishet erotica, women are always biting their lips while men flex their rippling biceps. In lesbian erotica, the same roles are recast with "butch and femme" couples. It's understood that all the erotica features only nondisabled, cisgender, white people, and that it centres penetration and multiple orgasms. Seamless sex with no mishaps, levity, or connection. I am so often looking for myself in sexual imagery, for people like me: people who have different bodies and abilities, who make mistakes and laugh at inopportune moments. I'm left wanting more.

More and more frustrated, surrounded by sex toys, candles, and a nearly empty bottle of whisky, I was worked up and wasted in all the wrong ways. So, in a spell of drunken sexlessness, I resolved that if you wanted something done right, you had to do it yourself. I would just have to write my own erotica featuring a person with a disability. Easy. I pulled out my laptop, and in half an hour I had written my very own erotica featuring a disabled person. Righteous and victorious, I published the piece to my blog and promptly passed out in my clothes.

A thing I had not considered when making this rash decision: on the internet, things spread faster than HPV.

When I woke up the next morning, I discovered that while I slept, my blog post had been read by almost eight hundred people. There was also a stern voicemail on my answering machine from my mother, reminding me that my grandmother is quite proficient at using the internet. As I emerged into daylight, I was certain I was receiving curious glances from strangers and friends alike. That weekend, at the market, a man I vaguely knew casually whispered that he was "interested in power play." That same night, I went to a dance party and received not one but three sexy propositions. Suffice it to say, the dry spell ended then and there.

It was a strange experience, unintentionally opening my bedroom door to countless strangers; it was as if they had all watched me writhing around, naked and sweaty. Luckily, the joy of having sex again trumped any sheepishness I was feeling about being such a sexualized extrovert. Plus, my aim in writing that piece of erotica had been to increase the representation of disabled people in sexual settings, and I now knew of at least one piece of erotica that involved a body like mine.

And so here it is again, the very piece of smut:

The bar was hot and crowded. Bodies pressed against bodies, beats pressed against ear drums, and all I wanted was for them to press me against the wall. I wanted to be held up and fucked. I wanted their hands to push against me so hard that they would leave marks. That feeling of being held up, thrown around, pressed on, and pried at until I am completely pliable—that's what I wanted more than anything.

"I need to go to the bathroom," I yelled up at them. The music carried my quiet voice away, and so I propelled myself forward, my wheels gently knocking their ankles so that they stumbled back a little, their ass falling against me. They were straddling my chair now, their weight on top of me, and even this contact, having their sweaty back pressed against my chest, our bodies still fully clothed, felt like too much. I wanted it so bad.

"I need to go to the bathroom," I said again, and to make my point clear, I pulled their earlobe into my mouth, drawing the soft skin between my sharp teeth.

They looked at me, obediently. They were as ready as I was.

People cleared a path for us as we went deeper into the bar. We reached our destination and entered the one-room wheelchair bathroom together. In situations like this, I sometimes wonder what people are thinking. Do they think my lover is only my assistant, helping me to transfer onto the toilet? Does anyone suspect that what we do in these private places and darkened corners is not always about my disability, but is most often about pure pleasure? We are usually fucking each other in these bathrooms, a thin wall separating us from the public. The people at the party outside have no idea what kind of highs we are reaching in these stolen moments, and their ignorance just makes me wetter.

We were alone together in the grimy room, and I wanted everything. I wanted it all, and all at once. I wanted them in my mouth, wanted them to cram their fingers down my throat with one hand while their other hand reached inside me. I wanted to feel full of them.

But I made myself wait.

Sweat had dripped down and pooled in my clavicle. "Lick it," I told them, and their rough tongue complied, scratching against my skin, making my cunt wet.

"Take my shirt off," and the silk was being pulled up over my head, exposing my tits to the hot, muggy air. My nipples were already hard, and they bent over me, pulling first one and then the other into their mouth.

"Now, put me..." I began, but they interrupted.

"No, my turn," they said.

We have this problem, the two of us. Two controlling people wanting to call all the shots, wanting to fuck and be fucked exactly the way we want, wanting to say how it's going to be. But sometimes I like being told what to do as much as I like doing the telling.

They didn't tell me what to do, but instead, made me do it, putting my body exactly where they wanted it, controlling me, contorting me. They lifted me out of my chair, and I was up against the wall. I held onto the bars, supporting myself with my arms. I can do this, but they know it makes me tired. They know that when they have me here like this, up against the wall and waiting, that they better fuck me and they better fuck me hard and fast until I am coming all over them, falling into their arms with the intensity of it all.

With one hand they pulled my hair, wrapping it tightly around their fist so my head was pulled to the side, exposing my neck for their teeth to bite into. With the other hand they pulled off my skirt. Their fingers slipped down and pressed against the soft cotton of my underwear. I could feel my clit throbbing beneath their touch. They must have felt it too, my body pulsing against them, and so they eased their fingers around my thong and against my lips.

They started gently, stroking me, teasing me. They knew I wanted them inside me, that I was impatient and waiting and aching for it, but they wouldn't give in right away. They kept it up, those subtle strokes, up and down, up and down, until I was so wet I was dripping on their fingers. My thighs were damp with my own juice and still they would not draw me open, would not reach deeper.

I couldn't take it.

"Baby," I said. "Baby, fuck me."

"Now?" they asked.

"Right now."

"*Right*, right now?"

"NOW."

"And if I don't?"

"You have to."

"I have to?"

"Yeah…"

"Tell me what you want."

"I want you to fuck me hard. I want you inside me up to your wrist."

"And what's the magic word?"

"NOW!"

They acquiesced. Part of them wanted me there all night, pressed against them and begging, but they also wanted to please me.

I felt their hand move my lips open. Their rough thumb stroked my clit, while their long, beautiful fingers reached down inside me. One finger, then two, then three, were in my pussy, circling. My cunt clenched around them. I wanted to swallow them up, wanted them never to leave my body.

My clit got harder and harder under their thumb. I know that they love this, love feeling how much my body wants them. And as they rubbed my clit, over and over, I expanded to take them in. My slit got wider and wider, and they slid all of themselves into me. Their wrist bone pressed up against my swollen sex. It felt like everything was happening all at once. My neck was in their mouth, my nipple twisted in between their fingers, my whole body riding their hand as it thrust into me, deeper and deeper. We moved together. I propelled myself against their body, forcing them further into me, driving them faster, and making them my own. They pressed harder and harder against my G-spot, working me. They are rough with me, but I can take it. Can take it and then some.

I began to tremble. My knees buckled. And then I crumbled. It felt too good. I felt too much. I couldn't stand any more. I fell forward, my soft tits pressed against their hard chest, while I gushed all over them. I came, and came, and it felt like I wouldn't stop coming, my body convulsing against theirs. My hair in their mouth, their neck against my lips, my cream wetting both of us, our sweat intermingled.

Finally, they stopped. They pulled out of me, and we stared at each other, not wanting to move, not wanting to end it.

Until there was a knock at the door.

They hurriedly helped me dress. In these moments I love their range of touch. That they can fuck me hard and fast, so good that it hurts, and then gently pull my shirt over my arms, zip my zipper, and put me into my chair.

We left the bathroom, cheeks flushed. The people outside smiled at us politely. I smiled back, and imagined that they were thinking, "What a trooper!" Often that's what people are thinking when they smile at me in a particular way. They don't know that my return grin means so much more, that I am laughing at them. They are about to use a bathroom that smells of my sex, flooded with my come.

The Tale of the Wooden Dicks

I am always half asleep at the Saturday morning farmers'
market. Bleary-eyed, I fondle the bags of greens and boxes
of berries. My breath is bad, and crud is all caught up in my
tear ducts. Often Friday night's mascara and lipstick remain
smeared across my cheeks and stale cigarette smoke ema-
nates from my hair. In short, I am not entirely alert on Saturday mornings. But I get up and roll downtown all the same,
no matter the conditions. This is in large part out of habit. I
have been going to the market for nearly a decade now. By
this point, my limbs move in that direction voluntarily.

The Wood-Working Woman has been there since the
beginning. Enter into the atrium of the big brick brewery
that houses the farmers' market and you will find her there,
laughing. She has been the first person I see on Saturday
mornings for the last nine years. A table full of beautifully
carved cutting boards, smoothed salad bowls, and ornate
soup spoons stands in front of her. Every weekend she
drives in from the South Shore to sell them. You'd think
she'd be tired and cranky, having gotten up at three-thirty
a.m. for her commute. But no, she is ceaselessly loud
and friendly. She yells a booming hello to me every week,
whether or not I want to talk. Her big, red face juts out,
smiling, over her wares, welcoming me to the day. She re-
minds me of both my mother and my bowel movements.

Like my mother, she is unselfconsciously beautiful and friendly. Like my shits, she is consistent, and experiencing her feels really positive.

Considering this relationship spans nine years, our exchanges have become predictable. We say our how-do-you-do's. We talk about the weather. I am hungry. She is caffeinated. We speak briefly, we smile, I move on. Always, it has gone this way. Or at least almost always, with the exception of one very significant deviation.

This digression from the norm happened on a morning that felt like any other. It was late July and oh so hot. I was sticky with sweat as I pulled open the heavy door to the market and sardined myself in with the mass of grocery shoppers and tourists. It was a summer of repetitive heat waves, and I was perpetually sticky as I hustled between two jobs. I would spend mornings slinging coffee for wealthy old people who would walk with entitlement off of cruise ships and demand a cappuccino. Come afternoon, I would change clothes and hobble in the heat up the hill to Venus Envy. From noon until evening, I slung not beverages but dildos, usually to a much nicer crowd.

But this Saturday was my day off, so I was sweaty but not working, groggy but not cranky, ready to eat and drink coffee and sit out back in the summer heat with my friends and do the weekend crossword. I eased my way deeper into the market, wiggling around older folks and baby carriages. As I reached the Wood-Working Woman, I found myself inadvertently jammed up against her table, momentarily trapped by the meandering crowd. I looked up and there she was, coffee in hand and smile on face.

"HI SWEETHEART, HOW YOU DOING?" she shouted at me cheerfully.

"Oh, just fine, same old," I replied. "How are you doing?"

"Well, I'm not complaining, but mostly because nobody'd listen."

"Fair enough," I smiled, as she laughed at her own oft-repeated joke.

"But I will say it has been too damned hot out there," she proceeded to complain happily.

I agreed, and we both nodded our mutual understanding. On a typical day, this would have been the point at which I moved on. But the mass of people had not shifted, and I was still trapped in one place, specifically in the place directly in front of her.

"So, what do you do?" The Wood-Working Woman asked pleasantly.

"Grmm, a bookstore," I mumbled.

Considering I had just started my job at the sex shop, I had not yet figured out how exactly to introduce my work. It would not be accurate to say that I was embarrassed, but I was often concerned that I would unintentionally make other people embarrassed. I could not yet gauge what was socially acceptable to say and what was not. So if someone seemed like an elder whom I should respect, or a person who was not comfortable talking about sex, I would use the old bookstore euphemism. It was not a lie exactly, just an omission. Not knowing much about the Wood-Working Woman, bookstore seemed like the safest bet.

"Oh, that is a nice job for a nice sweetheart like you. Which one?" she dug deeper.

"Downtown." I averted my eyes.

"Which one downtown?"

"Barrington Street," I answered begrudgingly. My cheeks were turning a bright pink.

"JWD Books?" She guessed.

"Nope."

"United Books?" The questions would not stop.

"No. Uh. No. Uh. Venus Envy." I gave in and told her. I was trapped.

I looked up to notice that her eyes had lit up and she was smiling broadly. Not the predicted reaction. She threw her head back, laughing. I offered a shrug. She reached her hands down, bending her knees and wordlessly sifting through her boxes of supplies. At the same time, the crowd closed in around me and I was shoved up closer, my hips pressed hard against the table. And then the next thing I knew there was two gigantic wooden penises being wielded wildly around my face.

"LOOK AT THESE FELLAS!" she said, in case I had some-how not noticed them. "I've been making these for years! They are very popular down where I'm from. Big sellers. I keep 'em under wraps in the city here for the children's sake. Gotta know a magic word to see 'em. I think they'd be a big hit though, at a store like yours. They shine up right nice and they are completely seamless. I carve 'em all by hand— big ones, small ones, little ones for your bum too."

I did not know what to say. I stared at the shining wooden cocks in silence.

"Well, whadda'ya think, sweetheart? Could they do well up here? This is the kinda thing you're dealin' with, isn't it?"

"Yeah, I mean, uh, that is my job. I, uh, I just, I, um, didn't expect you to be in this line of...uh...work," I explained. I still had not had a coffee. And I was flabbergasted.

"Hmph," she grunted, eyebrows raised. "You didn't think it was just you young city things who were up for a little fun, did ya?"

She had me. I had not presumed the South Shore of Nova Scotia to be a hotbed for wooden dildos. Clearly, I had misjudged.

She continued to extoll the virtues of wooden dongs for the next five minutes while I tried to politely absorb the things she was saying. My brain had been jolted awake by the double dicks in the face, but I was still unsure of how to respond. Clearly my concerns about making people uncomfortable had been pretty off the mark, at least in this instance. Was everyone so laissez-faire about sex? Were my feelings of shyness about my new job signs of naivety?

When she finally finished explaining her products, I walked away, impressed. My admiration for the Wood-Working Woman had quadrupled. Making your own dildos is a pretty rad move. While I never imagined carving cocks would be my primary activity, I resolved to be as proud and honest about my work as the Wood-Working Woman was.

Years later, I would be thoughtlessly whipping out dicks of my own to wield at unwitting grocery store clerks.

These things do happen.

10 YEARS LATER
2024

The Doctor Said

It's just a routine urinary tract infection, but my family doctor is booked up, so I go to the emergency room to get a prescription. I wait. I wait longer. Eventually, I am brought in to see the nurse. I give her my medical history in her own, abbreviated language: MVA (motor vehicle accident), SCI (spinal cord injury), 1995. Currently a UTI (urinary tract infection). Short, and to the point. She doesn't notice.

She asks about the car accident. How did it happen? How old was I? Who was driving? Did anybody die? My responses are short and to the point. Still, she does not notice. The interrogation goes on until the nurse arrives at her diagnosis: I am an inspiration, just so positive, especially considering my condition.

Later on, as tests are being administered, she asks if I would like for her to catheterize me. I decline.

My feet ache in a way I cannot describe. To try, it feels as though each joint has been soldered by a penguin. Which is to say, poorly. I am told that the wait time to see an orthopedic specialist in my home province is a decade long. Miraculously, I only wait for a year before he agrees to see me. I go alone and sit in a hospital room on the crepe paper that doesn't fit the examination table fully.

The specialist's resident comes in first. I give him my medical history in his own, abbreviated language—MVA in 1995, SCI, compression fracture at T4/5/6/11/12 vertebrae. He doesn't say much, just instructs me to wait for the specialist. I wait, continue to reposition the paper on the table, pilfer some latex gloves for later.

In time, the specialist comes in. He does not look at me directly, but he does grab my feet and pull them up to his nose. He touches my body without asking, warping my feet into unfamiliar positions. I fear his formidable nose hairs will graze my toes. He mutters diagnoses to the other man—collapsed arches, Morton's neuroma, metatarsalgia. When he's through discussing me as though I'm not in the room, he looks me in the face: "I can't cure you."

I remind him that I did not ask to be cured.

My life is being examined for legal purposes. Since the accident, I have had to allow a medical professional into my home to assess me, to judge my body's capacities, and to decide what kind of insurance benefits I am owed. Catheters, orthotics, canes, house-cleaning services. Do I really need these things, my insurance company wonders. So once a year, I spend an afternoon letting an occupational therapist follow me around while I do house chores. I answer questions about how I get dressed, how I bathe, how I make my bed. I explain that I live with my partner who helps with the housework: "She vacuums the floors; she shovels the driveway; she takes out the garbage." In her final report, the OT suggests that rather than employ a house cleaner, I get a mop with an extra-long handle— this seems illogical because it is—and writes that I live with a roommate who generously provides attendant care services. (I wish that I had responded with an email detailing the mechanics of scissoring.)

I am getting Botox injected into my bladder. As the urologist, nurses, anesthesiologists, and med students crowd around my splayed knees, trying to insert their paraphernalia into my urethra, my leg muscles begin their predictable contractions. My lower limbs flail wildly, making the doctor's work more difficult. I try to control my out-of-control body, but before I realize what has happened, a general anesthesia has been administered and I'm slipping under. My legs fall still. I am unconscious while they work on me. I wish that I had hidden a single grain of rice inside my urethra for them to find while I was knocked out, half-naked, and helpless. You know the rice I mean—those grains that come in tiny bottles with names carved into them. Janice. Matthew. Teresa. Mine would read "Trespassers Beware."

As I come to, monitors bleat out like robotic sheep. My vision is blurred, and I feel disoriented. The drugs have decimated all my tempered graces, and I am laughing, and crying, and asking the attending nurse too many questions. Words slip out, uncensored.

"Why was I given less anesthesia when I had an abortion than for this procedure?"

"Do you think about mortality more often because of your line of work?"

"Why can't I bring my partner into the OR with me, but the doctor can bring *all* of his med students? Considering that it is my cunt."

The nurse doesn't answer. The doctor walks in and congratulates me. The procedure went smoothly. He offers little more explanation and leaves before I get a chance to ask follow-up questions. As he walks away, I think about all of his layers of clothing—underwear, pants, T-shirt, sweater, socks, that long white coat.

In my mint-green hospital gown, my ass is cold.

In my wildest dreams, I can go to a doctor's appointment and not have to repeat the same abbreviated explanations for my body. I would be asked, first, "How are you feeling?" Then, "What can I do for you?" I would enter a clinic as whole and complete rather than as a puzzle to solve or a character to pity. In the hospital room, my body would be recognized as a humbling force rather than reduced to someone else's inspiration. Power would be redistributed. My expertise would be valued.

In the meantime, send me your bottled grains of rice.

(This piece is revised from the original, which first appeared in *No More Potlucks*, November 2015.)

Good Grief

I'm sitting in the chemotherapy unit at the Princess Margaret Cancer Centre. I know it's the best hospital in the country, but the waiting room has the same absence of personality as every hospital waiting room. The chairs are a stiff, burgundy faux leather, and the art features inspirational quotes about perseverance. I entertain myself by watching the receptionist, who I think of as Amy Sedaris. Her mask partially obscures her face, but her eyes and the way her body moves remind me so much of Sedaris that I feel a little starstruck every time she checks me in for my appointment. I like to imagine that she is about to break into an inappropriate *Strangers with Candy* bit at any moment.

Across from me is a woman who appears to be in her late forties, which I notice because most people here, other than me, are over sixty. She's sitting with another woman whom I presume to be an acquaintance because of the way the stilted conversation moves between them. They discuss what food options are available downstairs, or how their masks fit. The women don't settle into a familiar silence the way that my partner and I do. One of the women taps her foot anxiously against the dull linoleum floor. I think this must be her first time. A part of me wants to reach out to her and provide comfort, but I'm not sure what I would say.

"Some days, you will wait hours in this room while people

sleep and cry and get sick around you. Do not expect punctuality." Or "The gemcitabine will burn your veins regardless, but asking the nurse to add saline to the IV will help a little."

I decide these sound more like warnings than reassurances, and I say nothing.

Generally, the waiting room is full of camaraderie among the sick. Patients form relationships with one another and trade notes on their symptoms and progress. I overhear conversations about the loss of limbs, viral infections in stents, weeks to heal from cuts, and pleas to doctors for test results. It's a cacophony of collective anguish, a sound bath of suffering, and as it clamours against my ears, I can't deny that I too am sick, that I am dying. The grief that I set aside while I'm working in my garden or writing at my desk flares at the back of my throat.

In her cancer journals, Audre Lorde wrote:

I pretty much functioned automatically, except to cry. Every once in a while I would think, "What do I eat? How do I act to announce or preserve my new status as temporary upon this earth?" and then I'd remember that we have always been temporary, and that I had just never really underlined it before, or acted out of it so completely before. And then I would feel a little foolish and needlessly melodramatic, but only a little.[8]

This is the thing about learning that you will die. There are moments where the knowledge is so surreal, so painful, that it will make you feral. I have stuffed socks in my mouth to keep from screaming. I have wept hard enough

---

8 Audre Lorde, *The Cancer Journals* (New York: Penguin Classics, 2020).

to produce a nosebleed and let myself bleed unchecked all over my shirt at the doctor's office. Then, you come to realize that, of course, you're dying. I was already dying, was always going to die. We are all just "temporaries upon this earth." And you, I, feel sheepish about the histrionics.

In the early weeks after receiving my diagnoses, I booked myself a massage. Unsure how to tell my usual massage therapist that suddenly I was dying, I scheduled the appointment with a new therapist and filled out his intake form with the full details of my prognosis. I showed up for my appointment feeling like some kind of deity as I undressed, presenting my naked body as though it were holy. The masseuse chattered at me about the latest episode of *The White Lotus* while he worked the knots out of my shoulders. I agreed that Daphne and Ethan likely fucked.

In my work as a therapist, my clients taught me a lot about grief and I became skilled at witnessing and soothing theirs. I'll admit to being cliché and tell you that I often spoke in metaphors. Describing trauma and grief, I would tell clients that the traumatic events we have experienced live on inside our bodies, sometimes dormant but always there. When we go through a difficulty or a trauma in the present, the historic events get pinged, and the pain we previously endured comes alive again, influencing how we can tolerate or make sense of the here and now. I described this as a piano—the key plunked in front of you is what's happening right now, but if you look inside the instrument and you'll see a wire connecting to your past, taut and reverberating, *responding* to the present. When I think about that piano string now, I imagine it running up and down my spine, resounding inside my skin.

As I grieve for my life and for my coming death, and for the people I will leave behind, my oldest griefs are here too. I think often of the car accident and of what it has meant to live a disabled life. I have long been a celebrant of the joy of living in a queered body, and I have felt deep gratitude for the kind of self-knowledge that living in difference has afforded me. These emotions are true. The joy I feel about the circumstances of my life is a very active part of me. I live a great life! It's replete with deep friendships, meaningful relationships with plants and animals, and access to delicious foods. I've been alive during the development of the internet and the airing of *The Simpsons*, and I've witnessed what I think is going to be the beginning of the end of capitalism. I've gotten to watch every film of the *Scream* franchise come out in theatres, the good ones and the bad ones, and I've seen Alvvays play live. Pleasures abound! It's been, and I've had, a really good time.

But if I am honest, an ache lives alongside all of this. To be disabled is to experience exclusion and physical pain, oppression, stares and jeers. To live through a massive car accident and life-altering injury as a child is traumatic; it has given much, but it has also taken much away. For a long time, I was not able to acknowledge these points of suffering, afraid that they would subsume me. I lived only in disability pride, in a narrative of persevering without complaint. But I recently heard Leah Lakshmi Piepzna-Samarasinha lecture about disability justice, describing the process of grieving "not as an impediment or something to get over, but as a becoming."[9]

9 Leah Lakshmi Piepzna-Samarasinha, "Disabled Freedom Portals." Fordham 2022-2023 Distinguished Lecture on Disability, Fordham University, April 12, 2023, https://www.fordham.edu/academics/research/faculty-research/research-consortium-on-disability/events/fordham-distinguished-lecture-on-disability/2023-lecture/.

Leah said, "It can be a teacher. It can be something we are curious about and listen to. Viewing grief—feminized, disabled grief—not as a mess to be cleaned up but as a resource is disabled wisdom". At this point in my life, I am able to perform a sort of controlled emotional balancing act, to feel the grief alongside the joy, to tap into it as a resource. Finally, I am coming to understand that it's because of the grief that life's joy can feel more vibrant. In this way it's good, grief.

I write that as a therapist I "witnessed and soothed" the grief of others. These two things are one and the same—to be witnessed in your grief provides solace. To have another person take stock of the breadth of your suffering, to work to understand it, and to sit with you inside grief's parameters offers comfort. As a therapist, I never called myself a "healer" and scoffed a little at others who took up the term. By being with someone in their pain, by loving them through it, therapists provide merely a container for healing to occur. The client does the urgent work of healing, while the therapist only contains, witnesses, loves. I loved my clients, and watching the healing that occurred within our therapeutic relationship has been one of the greatest privileges of my life.

In sessions, I reminded clients that as humans we're just relational animals, no different than any other being on this earth. We need one another. Maggie Nelson, writing about Judith Butler, describes this by saying, "[We] are for another or by virtue of another, not in a single instance but from the start and always."[10] *From the start and always*. We have only ever existed within relationship. So now as

---

10 Maggie Nelson, *The Argonauts* (Minneapolis: Graywolf Press, 2016).

I explore the parameters of my own upending grief, I do it only and always with others. I feel all of my relations crowded around me, witnessing me and caring for me. I am learning anew that this is the only way to manage grief, to not bear it alone. I reorient myself to living and dying with cancer alongside my family, my friends, and my community. This practice is life giving. At the early stages of my diagnosis, I was reading a book about ecology by philosopher and biologist Andreas Weber, in which he describes the biosphere as follows:

> There is only one immutable truth: No being is purely individual; nothing comprises only itself. Everything is composed of foreign cells, foreign symbionts, foreign thoughts. This makes each life-form less like an individual warrior and more like a tiny universe, tumbling extravagantly through life like the fireflies orbiting one another in the night. Being alive means participating in permanent community and continually reinventing oneself as part of an immeasurable network of relationships.[12]

I have held this quote like a talisman, using it to remind myself that I am still an active participant in living, and that means I am never alone.

The nurse I think of as Amy Sedaris is discussing the progression of the seasons with a patient, an elderly man in a wheelchair. This model of time feels meaningless to me now, but I hold on to it, as time has become so elastic for

---

11 Andreas Weber, *Matter and Desire: An Erotic Ecology* (White River Junction, VT: Chelsea Green Publishing, 2017).

me. It's hopeful to remember that the crocuses and forsythia will soon bloom. I can also hear a woman whispering to her friend about her fears of chemotherapy. I concede that it does help to consider the seasonal, optimistic account of time paired with this patient's anxiety. I'll step into my own treatment today thinking about this dissonant twinning. Blooms and illness, grief and joy. The medicine that makes me ill offers healing. I'm in relation with it all. It cannot be denied. From the start and always.

Acknowledgements

Interpretation is never a static activity; very rarely does one story "stick" throughout a life. As we go along, we often find the stories we have been telling ourselves don't work any longer; we find we need to change them, so that they can do different work for us, accommodate new sets of knowledge and insight. It is in this sense that there is no such thing as a true story. This does not mean that all facts are fungible, nor does it mean that we don't each have a right to our own stories. It just means that the events of our lives will appear differently to us at different times.

—Maggie Nelson, *On Freedom: Four Songs of Care and Constraint*

I can't believe that *Hot, Wet, & Shaking* and this capsulized younger version of me has existed in the world for a decade. Even harder to believe is the fact that the opportunity to be in conversation with her arrived at the perfect moment, right as I was given ample room and reason to reflect on my life, my truths, my stories of myself. Rarely does a couple's therapist working through a global pandemic have the opportunity to step away from her clinical work; rarer still is she offered a book deal in the exact moment that she takes her leave. What kismet.

The stories in *Hot, Wet, & Shaking* have shifted over the years, and I am indebted to my publishers and editors, both then and now. They have corralled me into a legible shape, encouraged me in moments of writer's despair, and made room, as Nelson says, for my writing to "do different work." In 2014, Robbie MacGregor and Veronica Simmonds held my hands and promised me that I was deserving of a book. (I'm so grateful that this catalyzed my relationship with Veronica, who became one of my best friends.) In 2024, Norm Nehmetallah and Jules Wilson decided *Hot, Wet, & Shaking* deserved an updated and revised anniversary edition, and this decision was an unrivalled gift. Norm and Jules, at a time of great grief, you have both been exceedingly gentle with me while simultaneously urging me onward. If anyone reading this is an aspiring writer, I cannot speak highly enough about my time with Invisible Publishing. The best people; the most compassionate kind of support. I would also like to thank Christa Couture, who not only generously provided an afterword to this new edition, but has also championed my book from the very beginning. Christa, being in conversation with you over the years has both buoyed me and helped me feel things more deeply.

This book is about me, but it's also about Venus Envy. I probably spent over fifteen hundred hours—give or take—inside those four walls. Spending your twenties immersed in queer and feminist literature, surrounded by dildos and butt plugs, is a truly unparalleled experience. Education-based sex shops are changing the world, and it is not an exaggeration to write that Venus Envy changed mine, opening the expanses of what I thought was possible for myself. Thank you, Venus Envy, and everyone associated with it. There simply aren't enough words.

Many of the stories in this book take place in a particular moment in time—Halifax, from 2004 to 2014. It was a magic time to be young and living in a small, affordable city. Long Lake, Java Blend, the farmer's market, Gus' Pub, the speakeasy above Robert Street Social Centre, Charlie's, Tea Lake, The Khyber, the Fuller Lecture Series, and countless house parties. If you were there, you know what I mean. And if you were there, I owe you. We were all figuring out how to grow up (or how not to grow up), and I modelled myself after so many of you. I am a better dancer, a more hopeful activist, and a deeper friend because of our time spent together.

And finally, a huge thank you to my family, biological and chosen. In my writing, I hear my father's voice—so often my cadence parrots his, his straightforward way of communicating. My mother's warmth echoes through in how I relate to others. She has the rare skill of making anyone feel comfortable, and I mimicked this in my work at the sex shop (and then later as a therapist). My brother shows up in these pages as a wry smile—he taught me how to laugh at myself. And to my chosen family, who are too many to list by name—you each appear in this book as fireflies, orbiting one another, making up my community and the universe of my life. I don't exist without each one of you. I love you.

Afterword

"Dear Reader." So begins the very first page of *Hot, Wet, & Shaking: How I Learned to Talk About Sex*. It is an invitation to keep reading as though Kaleigh Trace wrote these pages directly to *us*. I accepted the invitation, and read on for an experience of honesty, humour, curiosity, and discovery. Any fan of Kaleigh's blog at the time, *The Fucking Facts*, would have known what they were in for, but I'd yet to encounter anything like it, what Kaleigh described as "Something that will make sense, something that will mean a thing or two to someone." From the first time I read *Hot, Wet, & Shaking* ten years ago, it has meant a great many things to me—and to others.

In sharing how she learned to talk about sex, Kaleigh shows us a critical, greater "how": how to pivot our lenses from those that centre the non-disabled, heterosexual, cisgender body, to those that centre ourselves, whatever our social location may be.

In my own experiences as a disabled, queer, cisgender, Indigenous woman, I have learned that very few people fit into the "ideal" that we have been socialized to elevate. Most of us feel—and are—different in some way. Most of us are excluded from mainstream narratives about bodies and sex. And I have learned that many of us have had to claw our way towards the tools and communities that can help us break free from those narratives.

Before #BodyPositive and #SexPositive were social media hashtags, before there were podcasts from most every lived experience to learn from, *Hot, Wet, & Shaking* was a guide to that freedom. Indeed, Kaleigh may have written the book she needed to read when she began looking to learn about sex on her own terms and found that what was available at the time excluded disabled bodies. So many texts about sex assumed that only non-disabled people were having it. And in content about disability, sex was left out. Kaleigh, in forging her own path of self-education and in turn sharing those lessons in *Hot, Wet, & Shaking*, was trailblazing. Ten years later, this book remains a lighthouse; and it continues to break ground.

When *Hot, Wet, & Shaking* was first published in 2014, it was both ahead of its time and long overdue. Ten years later, memoirs and personal essays (and actually every other genre) about sex remain lacking when it comes to disability, and books about disability are still catching up when it comes to the inclusion of sex. Kaleigh's voice is just as current and, unfortunately, just as needed as it was ten years ago.

Social media has become a source for education and community. And thank goodness—my love for my disabled body that began with reading *Hot, Wet, & Shaking* has only been deepened through witnessing and connecting with disabled content creators online. Yet, when hashtags like #HotDisabledSummer or #DisabledPeopleAreHot make the rounds on social media, or when you read comments on any posts from disabled influencers who dare to speak about sex, it's clear that ignorance about sex and difference is still rampant.

Education takes many forms, and the power of representation cannot be understated for those of us who live in difference and for those around us. Lack of representation contributes to shame, ignorance, and isolation. Ignorance can lead to dehumanizing others. In the case of our sexual selves, this ignorance also contributes to less pleasure, fulfillment, and empowerment.

The subtitle of *Hot, Wet, & Shaking* may well be "How I learned to talk about sex," but Kaleigh's identities as a disabled, queer, woman are inextricable from the conversation. A significant part of this book's impact for me personally was the disabled perspective. "I am in love with my body," Kaleigh writes. When I first read those words, I stopped. I realized I couldn't say the same about myself. I tried to read the line out loud with my own body in mind—my left leg is amputated above the knee, my scarred and bumpy stump a part of myself I grappled to accept for years. I had to whisper the words at first. I felt a longing, almost a need for permission, to repeat them. It had never occurred to me to love my disabled body. I had believed the narrative that disabled bodies cannot be as loved as non-disabled bodies, cannot be as valuable, cannot be as desired or appreciated. That simple statement was bold and life changing.

I would gush to friends and colleagues about the book. "Kaleigh talks about loving the shape of her legs, about pride in figuring out how to carry things in her teeth!" One of my closest, oldest friends got her own copy of *Hot, Wet, & Shaking*. As a non-disabled person, she also felt revelations of self-acceptance and exploration about her body. How beautiful that a love story to a disabled body is accessible to others! While the disability lens was most significant to me, a reader does not have to literally see themselves in Kaleigh's work to relate. This, too, is what makes *Hot, Wet, & Shaking* an enduring and relevant work. As Kaleigh says, "the most beautiful part of residing in difference is that you get to reconstruct everything we are told is truth."

In a book about how a person learned to talk about sex, Kaleigh gloriously lets us know that we are embarking on that journey from the position of compassion, care, and celebration. It is not the hard-won conclusion of the book; it is part of the thesis statement.

That care is one of the many generous aspects of Kaleigh's writing. Her candour, self-reflection, and humour achieve the brilliant effect of making the reader feel like a confidante; as the dear reader, you are kindred and trusted with some of Kaleigh's most intimate observations of her own journey. That trust is a gift, and it is our role to receive her experiences with care. Kaleigh doesn't assume we are ignorant or educated, but she does offer us the opportunity to be open. Without judgment or hierarchy, she brings us into her world to simply learn alongside her and to learn about ourselves.

These days, we may be used to, or at least exposed to, asking for and sharing pronouns, but in 2014, it was rare. I hadn't encountered the term "gender binary" before *Hot, Wet, & Shaking*, and when I encountered "they" for a stranger—because Kaleigh wouldn't want to assume anyone's gender—I paused, as that was a completely new concept to me. I learned. And I expanded. I'm so grateful for that lesson; it started my education about trans and non-binary people, which in turn created space in my life for allyship, friendships, and partners. As an artist, *Hot, Wet, & Shaking* also taught me something about how I wanted to write. I read Kaleigh's memoir before I wrote my own, *How to Lose Everything*. "What does a book about sex have to do with a book about grief?" a colleague asked. Openness; complexity; awareness; the sharing of pleasure and hurt without shame. Not to mention humour in some of life's most human moments. I learned what I wanted to give to a reader: a sense of being lifted up, celebrated, and supported in their experiences. A sense of connection; an example of community and possibility.

After devouring my library copy of *Hot, Wet, & Shaking*, I ordered multiple copies from my local queer bookstore to press into the hands of friends and family members. I hoped they too would laugh out loud, look inward, feel seen, and expand their understanding to see others more clearly. Invariably, they did. I still sing this book's praises and regularly recommend it. Kaleigh's stories have stayed with me all these years. The dirty laughs, the empowered truths, the moving vulnerability—I've thought of the bag of dicks, the post-brunch group of friends rallying to defend one of their own, the hot wheelchair-user fiction, and the daily acts of resistance as a queer and disabled person. I've thought of them often. Writing these words is an honour.

Dear reader, I hope we both continue to learn to talk about sex. I hope we continue to have conversations about disability, desire, worth, difference, and commonality with curiosity, gentleness, and a few juicy jokes. With Kaleigh's book in our hands, we have one of the best examples of how to do so.

—Christa Couture, 2023

Invisible Publishing produces fine Canadian literature for those who enjoy such things. As an independent, not-for-profit publisher, we work to build communities that sustain and encourage engaging, literary, and current writing.

Invisible Publishing has been in operation for over a decade. We released our first fiction titles in the spring of 2007, and our catalogue has come to include works of graphic fiction and nonfiction, pop culture biographies, experimental poetry, and prose.

We are committed to publishing writers with diverse perspectives. In acknowledging historical and systemic barriers, and the limits of our existing catalogue, we emphatically encourage writers from LGBTQ2SIA+ communities, Indigenous writers, and writers of colour to submit their work.

Invisible Publishing is also home to the Bibliophonic series of music books and the Throwback series of CanLit reissues.

If you'd like to know more, please get in touch: info@invisiblepublishing.com